A labour of love

A labour of love: women, work and caring

Edited by

Janet Finch and Dulcie Groves

Department of Social Administration
University of Lancaster

ROUTLEDGE & KEGAN PAUL
London, Boston, Melbourne and Henley

HQ
1106
L32
1983

First published in 1983
by Routledge & Kegan Paul plc
39 Store Street, London WC1E 7DD,
9 Park Street, Boston, Mass. 02108, USA,
296 Beaconsfield Parade, Middle Park,
Melbourne, 3206, Australia, and
Broadway House, Newtown Road,
Henley-on-Thames, Oxon RG9 1EN

Set in 10pt Century by Hope Services, Abingdon
and printed in Great Britain by Redwood Burn Ltd, Trowbridge

Library of Congress Cataloging in Publication Data

A Labour of love
Bibliography: p.
Includes index.
1. Women—Congresses. 2. Social policy—Congresses.
3. Social Service—Congresses. I. Finch, Janet.
II. Groves, Dulcie.
HQ1106.L32 1983   305.4   83-4469

ISBN 0-7100-9504-X (pbk)

Contents

Notes on contributors

Sally Baldwin is a Research fellow in the Social Policy Research Unit at the University of York, where she is engaged in DHSS-funded research into severe disablement in children, with a particular interest in the financial consequences of severe disablement. She has contributed to a number of publications on social security provision for disabled people and on the costs of disablement in children, and until recently was joint editor of the Yearbook of Social Policy.

Janet Finch is a lecturer in social policy at the University of Lancaster. Her current research interests are in marriage and family policy, with a focus on gender divisions. Recent publications include work on wives' incorporation in men's work, voluntary playgroups as preschool provision, education as social policy and (with Dulcie Groves) women and community care.

Caroline Glendinning is a Research Fellow in the Social Policy Research Unit at the University of York. She has undertaken research on the family consequences of severe disablement in children; on the impact of specialist social work services for children with disablement and their families; and on discrimination against married women with disabilities. She has written and contributed to publications on the non-contributory invalidity pension for married women; on the take-up of welfare benefits; and on families with disabled children.

Hilary Graham is a lecturer in social policy at the University of Bradford and currently is an Honorary Research Fellow of the Open University. Currently, her main research interest is in the impact of gender divisions on the health, and health care roles, of women. Recent publications also include work on mothers with young babies, and on research methodology.

Dulcie Groves is a lecturer in social policy at the University of Lancaster. Her research interests include pensions, income support for carers, financial consequences of divorce. With Janet Finch, she has developed an interest in women and community care, and has published on this topic.

Judith Oliver has spent most of her working life employed in the rehabilitation of the blind and in the welfare rights field. She is married to a tetraplegic and they have two children. She started the Association of Carers in 1981 as a response to the needs of carers whom she had met in her statutory and voluntary work.

Lesley Rimmer is an economist and was until recently a research officer with the Study Commission on the Family. She has researched and published on issues related to the family, public policy employment trends and the family, and single parent families.

Clare Ungerson is a lecturer in social policy and administration at the University of Kent. Her current research and teaching interests focus upon women's studies, and especially women and community care. She has published on this topic, and also on race relations and housing policy.

Alan Walker is a lecturer in social policy at the University of Sheffield and Honorary Secretary of the Disability Alliance. He is currently engaged in research into the family care of elderly people. Recent publications include work on ageing and community care, on disability, on unemployment, and on public expenditure and social policy.

Fay Wright began her career as a social worker with the elderly and handicapped, before moving into research and teaching in social policy. Until recently, she held an SSRC studentship at Bedford College, London, and has undertaken research into the care of elderly disabled parents by single daughters and sons.

Acknowledgments

The authors would like to thank all who have given help with this book and, not least, our contributors, who have been so prompt and helpful in the submission of their material. We are grateful to the Social Administration Association for funding a day conference on Women, Work and Caring at the University of Lancaster in November 1980 at which three papers were presented on which the chapters by Baldwin and Glendinning, Groves and Finch, and Walker are based. Dulcie Groves is also grateful to her late mother, Clarice E. Groves, a feminist, for various perceptive and humorous comments on the unwelcome dependencies of frail old age.

Introduction

This book focuses upon those hundreds of thousands of women who provide unpaid care outside of residential institutions—often in their own homes—for children and adults who are handicapped or chronically sick, and for frail elderly people.

Those for whom such women provide care are usually (though not invariably) relatives, and the care provided ranges from regular assistance with shopping or other household tasks for a person capable of servicing many of their own needs, to full nursing care as well as domestic services for someone who is totally incapacitated. The former type of situation can slide into the latter where care is being given to sick or elderly adults: children who are sick or handicapped from an early age may need 'total' care for the rest of their lives. Current government policies are geared towards such care being given 'by' the community. The aim of this book is to show the realities of this care at the present time.

Our interest is especially with those female carers who have given up paid work in order to provide care or who have never worked full-time because they, and/or other influential people in their lives, see such caring responsibilities as precluding paid employment. Likewise there are caring women who have significantly reduced their participation in their labour market. Caring women with little or no income from paid employment are in most cases either economically dependent on the income of another family member (usually male) or on state welfare benefits, or on some combination of the two. Meanwhile there are yet more women who struggle to combine 'caring' with a full-time job, often out of economic necessity and under considerable pressure to disguise their caring responsibilities whilst in the workplace. Such women include those with a strong commitment to women's financial independence and career development.

The central focus of this book, therefore, is upon the tension between women's economic independence (actual, potential or desired), and their traditional role as front-line, unpaid 'carers'. The contributions to this volume each explore different facets of women's experience of caring, the dilemmas which caring poses for women, the tension between paid work and unpaid caring (which can be hard work) and the social policy issues raised by the particular topics under discussion.

In the first section of this book, 'The social context of caring', Hilary Graham examines the concept of caring—what it means to care for someone, what is actually entailed, and the crucial position of 'caring' as an activity which permeates women's role both in the home and in the work-place. This theme is echoed by Clare Ungerson, who relates available evidence on women's economic activity to research findings on their domestic lives in an attempt to answer the question 'Why do women care?'

The second part of the book looks at the experience of caring. Sally Baldwin and Caroline Glendinning discuss the experience of mothers with disabled children with regard to the ways in which caring affects participation in the paid labour market. Judy Oliver, from her personal contacts as founder of the Association of Carers, comments on the situation of wives with disabled husbands, as reported by the women themselves. Fay Wright uses a field study of single men and women caring for elderly parents to analyse their employment and domestic situations, while Alan Walker highlights the nature of the dependencies which are implicit in caring relationships between elderly people and their caring relatives, and the ensuing conflict between women and the state, which itself helps to create such dependencies.

Our third section is concerned with the economics of caring. Lesley Rimmer examines the 'costs' of care, especially in terms of income foregone by female carers who give up paid employment. Finally, we ourselves discuss entitlement to invalid care allowance—the only state welfare benefit specifically targeted at 'carers', yet a benefit for which the vast majority of female carers remain ineligible.

In this introduction we draw out five themes which cross-cut the various contributions to this book and, in so doing, aim to signpost our readers through the book by highlighting some key issues about women, work and caring. Our first theme relates to the meaning of caring. In section 2, perceptive and sensitive accounts can be found of what it actually means to be a woman caring for a handicapped child, a disabled spouse or an elderly parent. Many of these experiences and meanings are shared by the very small number of men who are front-line carers in each of these categories. None the less there is something distinctive for a woman in being a carer, simply because 'caring' is an activity which is culturally defined as being 'natural' for women.

Ungerson demonstrates how important is the constitution of women as carers at the ideological as well as the material level. Not only does the state intervene at both levels, she argues: at the ideological level it actually promotes, through a range of policies, an ideal of family life in which women care for and nurture others. Graham's discussion contains a lucid and thoughtful account of the significance of 'caring' for the constitution of female identity. Caring, she suggests, is not only associated with women, but especially with those private places (principally the home and family contexts) where intimate relations with women are to be found. In its duality as both labour and love, caring defines 'what it feels like to be a woman in a male-dominated and capitalist social order'.

A further important feature of the meaning of caring which is common to several contributions to this volume is that caring means work. Although we have constituted the key tension as occurring between paid work and unpaid caring, this must not be allowed to mask the very important reality that 'caring' for a disabled or elderly person is indeed itself very hard work, whatever else it may be. The evidence for this contention is well illustrated in the contributions from Oliver, Wright and Baldwin and Glendinning. Its significance is discussed by Graham. The labour-intensive nature of the services which women provide for the sick, handicapped and elderly is often obscured in accounts which concentrate on the emotional and psychological aspects of caring. However, caring can never simply be reduced to 'a kind of domestic labour performed on people,' since it is always encompassed with emotional bonds. The fact that real, but unpaid, labour is hidden under the emotive rhetoric of 'caring' is part of the designation of women as the 'natural' carers. It is a singularly stark form of the assumption that women quite naturally have 'two roles', one of which is to engage in unpaid domestic labour.

Secondly, all the contributions in this book have to to be viewed in the light of the changing context of caring. In the first place, demographic changes in the second half of the twentieth century have altered both the composition and size of the various categories of dependants in need of 'care' and also the composition and size of the target groups of carers. Many of the handicapped children described by Baldwin and Glendinning will survive into a lengthy adult life, where once they would not have lived beyond childhood. The elderly people described by Wright and Walker have not only reached pensionable age but, especially if women, may well live on into extreme old age. Meanwhile, the single women described by Wright represent, thanks to higher marriage rates and a changed sex-ratio, a far smaller proportion of their age-group than was formerly the case, and are now outnumbered by their single men contemporaries. Married women tend to experience widowhood in middle or later life – a relatively small proportion predecease their husbands, thus obviating the risk of becoming one of the 'caring' wives so graphically described by Oliver. Meanwhile as Rimmer points out, divorce and remarriage are factors which must increasingly be taken into account in any discussion of caring. Rimmer, Ungerson and Graham bring into focus the 'caring' cycle which will in the future be faced by growing numbers of women who may find that they 'care' successively for children, elderly parents and a sick husband.

The other major aspect of the changing context of caring relates to change in the welfare state itself and especially what has been described as its 'restructuring' from the mid-1970s onwards. Not only has public social expenditure been sharply reduced, with the promise of further cuts to come, but the search is on for alternative bases for social service delivery which cast publicly provided services into an increasingly residual role. Such alternatives encompass not only provision by the voluntary sector and reliance on the 'informal' sector of welfare, but encouragement of occupationally based welfare and provision on a commercial and profit-making basis.

Of particular relevance to this book is the search for 'low-cost solutions' to the need for care of handicapped and elderly people, in the face of steep reductions in public expenditure and, in consequence, public welfare provision. Nor is the voluntary sector of service provision immune from the effects of economic recession. Low-cost solutions include a renewed enthusiasm for so-called 'community' provision of various sorts and a reliance on the recently designated 'informal sector' of welfare provision, that is—families, friends and neighbours who provide services for the dependent.

Rimmer queries whether such community care is in fact the 'low-cost' solution claimed for it, arguing that the true costs and losses have, up to now, been ignored. This point is echoed by Walker in relation to community care and the elderly. In emphasising the marginal position of women in the labour force, he notes the absence of public discussion of the costs borne by women – the designated 'carers' who are viewed as a species of wage-earner who can, if necessary, be detached from the paid workplace, without (as Groves and Finch demonstrate) any income support for the vast majority of such women. The continued denial of invalid care allowance to most female carers epitomises care 'by' the community as a cost-saving device.

Both demographic change and the 'restructuring' of the welfare state have been grafted on to a pre-existing situation in which women have been defined as the 'natural' carers and also as the dependants of men. These alleged characteristics of women make them especially attractive as potential providers of unpaid care, in the private domain to which they have traditionally been assigned. Such features are however in no sense inevitable facts of human existence. As Ungerson argues, the designation of women as carers is a social construct at the level of ideology, which has also concrete material implications. It is important therefore to recognise that, like other socially constructed features of our lives, these processes are capable of being changed.

Our third theme relates to choices in caring. In many cases women faced with a perceived need to care (their own or some other person's perception) feel that they have absolutely no choice whatsoever but to 'carry on caring'. This point is plainly made by Ungerson. None the less, she finds it useful to consider the 'opportunity costs' of women's participation in the labour market as an addition to their domestic work. Ungerson shows that women's economic activity is limited by a strong, imposed set of beliefs that they 'really *ought* to be doing good for their families back home'. Such beliefs can of course produce guilt in women who, for whatever reason, are not producing front-line care themselves. To take a rare example, we suspect that even in a situation where there are the financial resources to purchase top-quality residential care for a very frail elderly parent who positively wants to live in a good nursing home, it is more than likely that a daughter will feel guilty if such a choice is exercised—and not least if it is her own high earnings which are instrumental in making such a choice possible.

There is clearly an important distinction to be made between caring which is entirely substituted for paid work and caring which is to a greater or lesser extent combined with paid work. In the first instance, the fact that caring may necessitate the actual giving up of paid work is recognised by the provision of a publicly provided cash benefit—the invalid care allowance, which is available to men and to single (non-cohabiting) women who actually give up paid work in order to provide what might be termed 'full-time care' for a disabled person. As Groves and Finch show in their chapter, the fact that most women are ineligible for this benefit implies that they are deemed to be not in need of 'independent' financial support, because they are presumed to be the dependants of men. The 'choice' between paid work and 'unpaid' caring is, in other words, treated as a very different issue for men, as contrasted with women.

The immense seriousness of taking a decision to give up paid work is well illustrated in Wright's contribution where men and women alike, as 'self-supporters' (some no doubt assuming additional financial responsibilities for those for whom they are caring) are seen to endeavour to keep their paid employment for as long as possible. The male carers, however, mostly had assistance which enabled them to stay at work, whereas the women mostly did not. Similarly the mothers of handicapped children studied by Baldwin and Glendinning regarded the opportunity to engage in paid work as very important (if temporary) escape from the 'daily grind' of housework and caring which constituted the rest of their lives.

Where work and caring are combined, the two are constantly in tension, as Wright's study again makes clear. Because paid work is mostly organised around the lives of men, few allowances are made for employees who may also have responsibility for the care of a highly dependent relative. This means that women who by choice or necessity attempt to combine work with caring often, as Rimmer illustrates, reduce their hours of work or restrict their employment opportunities in order to accommodate their 'caring' responsibilities. Wright points out that most of the women in her sample had been in 'secure white-collar jobs': some had given up their jobs but others resorted to a variety of strategies, including part-time work, and variations on the use of 'flexitime', in order to continue with paid work. This evidence raises issues around a possible reorganisation of paid work, in ways which would more easily accommodate 'carers' as employees, a point to which we return.

Consideration of the tensions between paid work and unpaid caring leads naturally into our fourth theme—the costs of caring. The contributions by Wright, and by Baldwin and Glendinning spell out in some detail the financial costs of caring in certain specific contexts. The parents in Baldwin and Glendinning's study were propelled into poverty by a situation which precluded earnings via 'two incomes' or even via one earner topping up wages by overtime. The 'sole bread-winners' described by Wright were in some cases foregoing not only current earnings, but occupational pension contributions. Both examples highlight not only the inadequate income replacement currently available to carers, but also, as Walker points out, make the link between poverty during the 'working' adult years and poverty in old age. The low level of available income support and its denial to most of these very people—women, who bear the brunt of the caring—raises a question about the extent by which the current government's predilection for 'informal care' will be matched by adequate income support for 'carers'. Such support needs to take on board those social and demographic changes discussed by Rimmer and the marriage-like relationships which feature in the chapter by Groves and Finch.

The concrete, financial costs of caring are paralleled by the equally important—if less measurable—personal costs, some of which are graphically illustrated in Oliver's chapter on caring wives. For such women, the 'for better or worse' clause in the marriage vows takes on an especially stark meaning. The assumption that a wife will always be present means that many get little or no support from outside the home. The impact is felt in terms of isolation, lack of friends and feelings of being 'de-sexed'. The mothers of handicapped children also experience considerable isolation, not unrelated to the lack of opportunity to do paid work, as pointed out by Baldwin and Glendinning. The pain of isolation from paid work is also evident from Wright's account of single-women carers who had given up outside employment and who, in the absence of male partner, children or paid job, occupy a position unusual among their contemporaries—one shared by few men. Graham's discussion provides a penetrating account of the dilemmas of providing care which comprises both labour and love. Caring, she argues, demands the adoption of a life-style which isolates the carer from the outside world. It is a privatised form of labour and something which women invariably do alone: yet, at the same time, it is the medium through which women are accepted into and feel they belong in the social world.

Finally, the theme of alternatives to present modes of caring is implicit in a number of contributions to this book. Any attempt to look into the future is bounded by a utopian perspective on the one hand, and a realistic perspective on the other. The two perspectives seem to point in very different directions.

Realistically, the situation for women as carers (actual

and potential) seems likely to get very much worse in the immediate and foreseeable future. Further shifts away from publicly provided welfare services seem likely and it is plain that they will be in the direction of further reliance on 'the community' and on 'the informal sector of welfare'. The Conservative government has made this clear and meanwhile the Barclay Report on social workers, in arguing for the development of 'community social work' offers a model of partnership between personal social services and 'community' which clearly equates 'community' with informal care. While Barclay posits 'shared caring' between statutory services and informal carers, public expenditure cuts make it unlikely that carers will get much support in practical terms from local authority social service departments or yet from voluntary organisations reliant on public funds.

Taking a more utopian stance, it can be asked whether it is possible to envisage a future in which the care of elderly and handicapped people is provided in a radically different context, which does not depend mainly on the unpaid labour of women. In other words, is it possible to develop a non-sexist form of caring? We can only be brief and speculative on this point, but we do think that there are a number of avenues which merit further exploration.

Already there is considerable interest in the 'reorganisation of work', which appears to stem partly from a wish to redress the traditional unequal division of labour as between men in the workplace and women in the home, and partly from a desire to share out scarce paid work more fairly. Work-sharing is one strategy advocated in these contexts and is attractive in the 'caring' situation, provided that it offers of itself, or in combination with some non-discriminatory form of income support, an income which is well above the poverty line. There would also seem to be useful potential in notions of 'caring leave' or part-time employment opportunities which include guaranteed measures of employment protection especially designed for 'carers'. However, the choice of full-time employment should be available, which necessitates provision of good domiciliary support which does not itself exploit women as low-paid care-givers. We suggest that residential care of high quality, which avoids 'institutional' overtones, may in some cases be a preferred alternative to what could amount to saturation by domiciliary services. Our preference is for a restructuring of the economy which would enable such services to be publicly provided.

In envisaging such a future, we are very aware that many discussions of caring push to the periphery the demands of those who are being cared for. The glib assumption that care 'in' the community or 'by' the community is inherently better than residential care has to be judged against the context of a long history of poorly provided residential institutions, with little opportunity for independent lives to be led within them. Even if most elderly people do now say that they do not want residential care, this does not mean that they would never want it, if care of a very different sort were to be offered. Nor is it the case that parental care is inevitably going to be a preferred alternative for the care of all handicapped children—it almost certainly is a preferred alternative to much of the under-resourced institutional care currently offered.

It can be argued that handicapped and elderly people may not wish to collude with policies which force them to be cared for in the homes of close relatives. Blood ties do not guarantee that such informal care is an optimal situation—far from it. As indicated by the contributions to this book, where public policy virtually dictates such care, the labour of love can very quickly become labour quite devoid of any of the feelings of affection which are meant to be its cornerstone.

PART 1

The social context of caring

CHAPTER 1

Caring: a labour of love

Hilary Graham

Introduction

This chapter examines what caring means and what caring entails. Clearly, what it means to care for someone and what it entails are closely related, but they are not synonymous. The two aspects are distinguished at the outset because both need to be confronted and confronted together, if we are better to understand the nature of caring in Western society.

Caring is not something which can be neatly defined, not even by the redoubtable Oxford dictionary. However, in broad terms, it is a concept encompassing that range of human experiences which have to do with feeling concern for, and taking charge of, the well-being of others. This definition alerts us immediately to the question of meanings and entailments: 'feeling concern' and 'taking charge' have both psychological and material implications. As the chapters in this book testify, the experience of caring touches simultaneously on who you are and what you do.

Caring, although a difficult concept to define, is clearly a central one for social policy. On the one hand, the experience of caring and being cared for is intimately bound up with the way we define ourselves and our social relations. On the other, caring is an integral part of the process by which society reproduces itself, and maintains the physical and mental health of its work force.

Recognising these two dimensions is central to the analysis presented in this chapter. It suggests that caring demands both love and labour, both identity and activity, with the nature of the demands being shaped by the social relations of the wider society. In gender-divided societies like ours, caring tends to have particular consequences for the identity and activity of women.

Recognising the multi-dimensional nature of caring is relatively straightforward: it is building an analysis around it which is the problem. Whether defined as an identity or an activity, the experience of caring slips between the tight conceptual categories of the social sciences. Such categories were fashioned for the new social relations of nineteenth-century capitalism, social relations built upon changes in the organisation of caring. Yet, significantly, they obscured both these changes in the rearing of children, in household labour, in the care of the sick and the old, and the underlying system of gender divisions on which the new patterns of caring were based. As Margaret Stacey has noted, a conceptual framework which separates reproduction from production, private from public, home from work, leisure from labour will inevitably fail to confront experiences which transcend such divisions (Stacey, 1981).

The nature of caring, and the nature of the concepts through which social scientists have comprehended it, constitute two distinct but related problems which this chapter attempts to tackle. It has to face, firstly, the fact that caring is simultaneously about our material existence and about our consciousness. It has to face, secondly, the deficiency of a scientific apparatus which is blind to the very phenomena we wish to make visible.

It is problems such as these that feminist analysis seeks to overcome. Building upon the shared experiences of women, it has begun to uncover—and to make sense of—phenomena which have remained 'hidden from history' (Rowbotham, 1973; Smith, 1974). Much of this work—on family relationships and family responsibilities, on the impact of children and the onset of old age—bears directly on the question of caring (for example, Leonard Barker and Allen, 1976; Mitchell and Oakley, 1976; Burman, 1979).

These studies suggest that, whatever the problems professionals face when talking about caring, it is a term which permeates our ordinary accounts of everyday life. It structures our conversations about our friends and lovers: it is central to the way we think about our family (Stacey and Price, 1981, p. 186). Conversations, too, about encounters with the welfare state, as workers and as clients, are often conversations about caring (Jordan, 1976, chapter 5).

Working from and within this everyday familiarity with the concept of caring, the chapter advances its argument in four sections. The first section defines the everyday experience of caring as a labour of love. The next two sections examine the way in which social scientists have represented the love and the labour of caring, the second section drawing from the psychological literature and the third section outlining some of the insights provided by recent research within social policy. The final section, summarising the contributions and limitations of these two approaches, lays out some ground-rules for the construction of an alternative analysis of caring.

Caring: a labour of love

Everyday conversations about caring are generally recognised to be conversations about feelings. When we talk about 'caring' for someone, we are talking about our emotions. Where the word 'love' seems inappropriate, we choose the words 'care for' to convey a sense of the bonds which tie us to our friends, our lovers, our children, our parents, our clients, our patients.

Caring, in this sense of feelings, is seen as a basic human emotion. All normal people want to, and expect to, experience it. 'Caring too much' may be, as the song says, 'just a juvenile fancy' but none the less, as another tells us, we all want 'someone, somewhere, someone who'll care (and take a chance with me)'. Although a universal need, only certain social relations are seen to facilitate the giving and receiving of care. In general, caring relationships are those involving women: it is the presence of a woman—as wife, mother, daughter, neighbour, friend—which marks out a relationship as, potentially at least, a caring one. As those involved with the handicapped and the elderly know, caring—whether in the home, the community or the hospital—depends upon

women (Doyal, 1979; Finch and Groves, 1980; Parker, 1981).
Male relationships, by contrast, are seen to be mediated in a
different way, with the bonds—ostensibly at least—based not
upon compassion but on competition (Chodorow, 1978).

Caring tends to be associated not only with women, but
with those private places where intimate relations with
women are found. Specifically caring is associated with the
home and family. As Margaret Stacey and Marion Price note,
'the values of tenderness and care are present and are permis-
sible in the family more than elsewhere' (1981, p. 180). By
contrast, relations contracted within the labour-market are
seen to engender a degree of social distance incompatible
with the giving of care. There are exceptions, of course;
occupations where 'the woman's touch' has been formally
incorporated into the job specification. These occupations,
interestingly, have a special designation: they are the 'caring
professions' in which the workforce is largely female (Oakley,
1981, pp. 155–8). In nursing, social work and primary school
teaching, social relations are mediated through care, with, as
Margaret Adams points out (Adams, 1971, p. 558):

> the synthesizing function traditionally discharged by
> women . . . translated to a wider sphere beyond the home
> . . . Instead of (or in addition to) keeping the family intact
> and maximally functional, women become involved in
> housekeeping tasks on behalf of society at large.

The image of caring-as-feelings clearly speaks to an important aspect of our experience. We *do* care for a few people in a
way which is different from the more instrumental relationships dominating most of our lives. But it is not feelings alone
which distinguish these special relations. Caring involves the
transaction, too, of goods and services. The caring relationships women enter into—with husbands, children, parents,
clients—are built on material as well as symbolic bonds.
Caring, as carers have testified through history, is experienced
as a labour of love in which the labour must continue even
where the love falters (*Oral History*, 1977; EOC, 1981;
Spring Rice 1981).

The dual nature of caring—as labour and as love—is
reflected in the social science literature. However, here the

two dimensions are treated separately. The material aspects of caring have been studied (albeit only recently) within social policy: psychologists, meanwhile, have explored its emotional significance. This disciplinary division has certain advantages. By highlighting the labour involved in caring, it has been possible to quantify the economic contribution of the caring role (EOC, 1981; Nelson, 1980). Recent research has documented how this role locks both carer and cared-for into positions of dependency, positions which the welfare state serves to institutionalise rather than alleviate (Walker, 1980; Finch and Groves, 1982). Meanwhile, psychological research has uncovered the emotional consequences of caring. Psychologists, of disarmingly different political persuasions, concur that caring is not just another work-role carved up for women in the sexual division of labour. Caring, they contend, is the constitutive activity through which women achieve their femininity and against which masculinity takes shape (Horney 1932; Baker Miller 1976; Chodorow, 1978). Any material contribution that caring might make to the maintenance of capitalism and patriarchy is thus seen as incidental to its role in the construction of women's psychology.

The disciplinary separation has inevitable limitations, however, narrowing both the range and depth of our understanding. The psychological perspective sees caring as the mechanism through which the consciousness of women and men is recreated generation by generation: but as a result, it has tended to ignore the economic and political forces which determine that consciousness in the first place. Conversely, within social policy, the opposite tendency is detectable, with psychology subordinated to economics. Caring, stripped of its symbolic role in the construction of women's identity, is reduced to the obligatory transaction of goods and services which occurs within the patriarchal family. Caring, here, tends to be defined as an act of female sacrifice and supreme selflessness, not, as many psychologists would argue, as the primary process through which both a sense of self and a sense of self-fulfilment is achieved.

Caring as women's nature: psychological perspectives on caring

This section outlines some of the psychological literature which addresses, directly or indirectly, the role of caring in gender socialisation. It is necessarily highly selective, aiming to indicate directions and tendencies within work on women's psychology rather than providing an authoritative account of work in the discipline as a whole.

Central to the psychological paradigm is the view that caring can not be reduced to a labour process — a problem inherent in recent attempts to categorise and qualify the components of caring (see EOC, 1981, and Parker, 1981). Its significance lies instead in its psychological affinity with femininity; in the fact that the qualities demanded of care-givers — a sensitivity to the needs of others, an ability to wait, watch and adapt as these needs change — are the qualities displayed by women in Western society.

This intimate relationship between caring and femininity is viewed not simply as an aspect or outcome of the sexual division of labour within the family. It is, Horney and De Beauvoir would argue, the organising principle around which it is built (Horney, 1932; De Beauvoir, 1972). 'Caring' becomes the category through which one sex is differentiated from the other. Caring is 'given' to women: it becomes the defining characteristic of their self-identity and their life's work. At the same time, caring is taken away from men: not-caring becomes a defining characteristic of manhood. Men are marked out as separate to and different from women because they are not involved in caring for (and with) others. Their sense of self is achieved by doing things for (and by) themselves (Chodorow, 1978).

The suggestion that caring is the concept which marks the boundaries between female and male is embodied in the psychologists' distinction between 'being' and 'doing' (Chodorow, 1971). 'Being' is a concept which encapsulates the other-directed but essentially passive nature of femininity; 'doing', conversely, captures the self-directed and active nature of masculinity. According to Karen Horney, for example, femininity is something a woman acquires through her sexual relations with men — and specifically through copulation, conception and childbearing. In this relationship, 'she performs her part by merely *being*, without any doing' (1932, p. 359, italics in original). Masculinity, by contrast, must be actively achieved: the mechanics of sex and reproduction demands that 'the man has to *do* something in order to fulfill himself' (ibid., italics in original). Simone de Beauvoir and Margaret Mead see the division between 'being' and 'doing' reflected in social as well as the sexual arena. De Beauvoir notes, somewhat ruefully, that the young boy enters into the public domain to do productive work and become wealthy ('he will be a seaman or an engineer, he will . . . go away to the city, he will see the world, he will get rich, he will feel free', 1972, p. 325). Meanwhile his sister remains within the restrictive private domain, condemned to a non-productive life of inactivity chosen not by herself, but by others.

> The young girl will be a wife, a grandmother; she will keep house just as her mother did, she will give her children the same care she received when young—she is twelve years old and already her story is written in the heavens. She will discover it day after day without ever making it.
>
> (De Beauvoir, 1972, p. 325).

Mead develops a similar argument, but stresses the costs as well as the benefits accruing to men. Women's caring role gives them a 'simple sureness' in their sexual identity, while masculinity has to be 'kept and re-earned every day'. As a result, boys, unlike girls, live in fear of becoming 'unsexed by failure' (Mead, 1949, p. 303).

Although highlighting the obvious differences in the life-styles and life-chances of the sexes, these explanations of women's psychology reproduce many of the ideological assumptions we need to question. A typology which separates doing from being, working from caring, represents little more than reworking of the traditional distinction between men-who-make and women-who-mend. According to this tradition, men are defined through their relation to the labour market, by specifying their occupation (or lack of it). Women, by contrast, are introduced in less universalistic terms, through their caring relationships—as Bill's wife and Ben's mother. As George Eliot put it in *The Mill on the Floss*, 'you don't ask what a lady does, you ask who she belongs to.'

However, instead of questioning this traditional division of labour, psychologists have tended to base their analyses upon it. As a result, they misrepresent and trivialise the nature of women's role. Caring and femininity are defined within the narrow confines of marriage and motherhood, where women are seen to achieve their state of being through their relationships with their husbands and children. However, women's dependent status is determined by economic as well as psychic forces; forces which extend beyond the marital home into a network of caring relationships within the extended family and the community (McIntosh, 1981, and the chapters in this volume by Walker and by Groves and Finch). A woman's experiences and identity as a carer are increasingly moulded not through her involvement with the able-bodied members of the immediate nuclear family but through the services she provides for the sick, the elderly and the handicapped (Parker, 1981; EOC, 1982a). A theoretical model which explains women's predisposition to care in psychological terms inevitably masks the possibility that it is not a product of an enduring feminine personality, but results from the particular way in which reproduction (in its broadest sense) is organised in our society.

Secondly, psychological accounts obscure the labour-intensive and highly stressful nature of the caring role. For example, like Simone de Beauvoir, Margaret Adams, in an otherwise-excellent account of women's psychology, argued that caring locks women into 'self-defeating trivialities' which deprive society of 'the vital and significant contributions that women might make' (Adams, 1971, p. 536). However, as empirical studies testify, caring—whether for husbands and children, or for those outside the nuclear family—is far from trivial and insignificant. It is moreover, an activity where questions of success are constantly raised, and women can indeed feel 'unsexed by failure' (Graham, 1982).

The distinction between 'doing' and 'being' misrepresents the nature of women's caring role in a third way. It masks the way in which the categories through which we define gender are social constructs and not psychological entities. What counts as caring is determined as much by who does it as by what is done. Non-work labels, like 'child care' and 'keeping house', tend to be attached to the contributions which those in subordinate positions make to society: 'work' and, in particular, 'skilled work' are terms reserved for the activities of men. As Anne Phillips and Barbara Taylor note, such labels should be seen as ideological categories 'imposed on certain types of work by virtue of the sex and power of the workers who perform it' (1980, p. 79). None the less, caring remains unique in largely remaining outside commodity production, as a form of labour with only limited possibilities for the specialisation and mechanisation on which profit-making depends.

Jean Baker Miller and Nancy Chodorow have attempted to provide alternative perspectives on caring which take account of the ideological and economic context in which it occurs (Baker Miller, 1976; Chodorow, 1978). Baker Miller, for example, suggests that it is through their subordinate position that women acquire their psychological predisposition to care: female sensitivity, empathy and compassion are qualities finely adapted for survival in a male-dominated society. Women 'become highly attuned to the dominants, able to predict their reactions of pleasure and displeasure. Here . . . is where the long story of "feminine intuition" begins' (Baker Miller, 1976, p. 11). Although devalued, Baker Miller suggests that these are qualities on which a more caring society can be built (1976, p. 57):

> Women have traditionally built a sense of self-worth on activities that they can manage to define as taking care of and giving to others. If they can convince themselves that they are doing a good job that can be defined in this way, then they can accomplish tremendous things.

Nancy Chodorow adopts a more explicitly psychoanalytic approach. Unlike Baker Miller, she argues that the caring role is not reproduced directly through the processes of male domination. It is reproduced by women themselves, through the dynamics of the mother–daughter relationship. In caring for children, women recreate the personality types we associate with masculinity and femininity. The care a mother gives her daughter lays down the needs and capacities for her to care for others in later life. The care she gives her son produces the personality characteristics needed for participation and success in the uncaring world beyond the home (Chodorow, 1978, pp. 167, 160):

> Girls emerge . . . with a basis for 'empathy' built into their primary definition of self in a way that boys do not. Girls emerge with a stronger basis for experiencing another's needs or feelings as one's own. From very early, because they are parented by a person of the same gender, girls come to experience themselves as . . . more continuous with and related to the external object-world. . . . Boys come to define themselves as more separate and distinct, with a great sense of rigid ego boundaries. The basic feminine sense of self is connected to the world, the basic masculine sense of self is separate.

In Chodorow's account, as in Baker Miller's, caring is identified as an activity intimately connected to the male-dominated society in which it is embedded. (As Chodorow notes, 'the sexual division of labour and women's responsibility for child care are linked to and generate male dominance', 1978, p. 214.) However, problems still remain. Caring can not be explained wholly in terms of psychodynamics—whether located within the mother–child relationship (Chodorow) or the relationship between dominant and subordinate (Baker Miller). The caring role has more complex origins. It is constructed through a network of social and economic relations, within both the home and the workplace, in which women take responsibility for meeting the emotional and material needs not only of husbands and children, but of the elderly, the handicapped, the sick and the unhappy. Further, as Janet Sayers argues, psychological accounts of women's role tend to assert not simply the value of caring but the value of femininity itself, an assertion which can quickly slip into an acceptance of the popular assumption that women and men enjoy 'equality in difference'. In so doing, they encourage a celebration of the ideological arrangements which support women's subordination (Sayers, 1982).

Caring as women's work: social policy perspectives on caring

A reconception of caring is central to the contemporary reconstruction of women's psychology. It is central, too, to the broader project of developing a feminist perspective on women's position in society. The key to such a perspective is seen to lie in an understanding of the nature of the family (McIntosh, 1979). Here, the concept of caring is regarded as fundamental in two respects. Firstly, as the previous section indicated, caring-by-mothers is identified as the process by which the construction of gender takes place: it is the way men and women emerge as different kinds of human beings. Secondly, caring-by-wives-and-mothers is seen as the mechanism by which families are reconstituted on a daily basis. It is the provision of high quality and unpaid care within the home which keep the family going. These two dimensions, the construction of gender and the maintenance of the family, are closely interrelated. The family—or, more precisely, the gender categories of husband, wife, son, daughter, grandfather, grandmother which make up the family—is sustained by the caring-work of women. This family unit, in turn, provides the structure in which caring is carried out: in which children are nurtured, husbands sustained, and the elderly and handicapped supported.

While psychologists explain the sexual divisions within the family in terms of psycho-dynamic needs, feminists working within social policy see the division between men-who-do and women-who-care as reflecting the needs of the wider society. The social forces at work, however, are complex and cross-cutting. The social and spatial separation of production (doing-in-the-workplace) from reproduction (caring-in-the-home) is linked to the rise of capitalism and its attendant separation of 'breadwinners' and 'dependants'. However, the logic of capitalism alone does not explain why these divisions coincide with those of gender (Breugel, 1978; Hartmann, 1979). It does not explain why caring should be 'women's work', why the home should be 'women's place', why women should be appendages and men their breadwinners. To understand the 'gendered' nature of caring, we need to confront the pre-existing sexual division of labour on which and in which the new forms of economic organisation developed.

Where this is done, hidden dimensions are revealed within our social world (Leonard Barker and Allen, 1976; Land, 1978). The institutions most centrally involved in caring— the family, the community and the state—take on a different form. They emerge not as monoliths, solidly uniform and sexless, existing 'out there' in the social fabric, but as social structures which carry within them the class and gender relations of a social order which is both capitalist and patriarchal. 'The family', for example, long seen by social scientists as the privatised form of care necessary for 'the economy' to function efficiently, is recast not simply as the setting for group consumption within capitalist societies, but as the locus of gender struggle (Hartmann, 1981). Individuals within the family are redefined both as family members, sharing a unity of interests, and as members of gender categories with different and often competing interests. Thus, family life for men may well provide an identity which frees them from the alienation they experience at work. For women, this alternative identity often proves less liberating since it is achieved only by subjugating themselves to the needs of their family (Foreman, 1977).

Similarly the concept of dependency, although carrying no apparent gender-tag, has a very different meaning for men and women. Dependency is seen as a condition created through the processes of capitalist expansion, in which increasing sections of the population are displaced from the labour market to rely for their livelihood upon the family and the state (cf. Walker, in this volume). However, like the concepts of the family and the state to which it is crucially linked, the nature of dependency can not be understood in isolation from the sex-gender system. Some categories of dependent children, for example, receive care and support but give no tangible benefits in kind. However, for women, the experience of dependency is more contradictory. Their dependent status—as housewives, mothers, dutiful daughters—is not absolute, but is conditional upon their being simultaneously depended upon by others. Thus, for many women, being a dependant is synonymous not with receiving care, but with giving it (Finch and Groves, 1982). For children, and for men, economic dependency and poverty is the cost of being cared for: for women, economic dependency and poverty is the cost of caring.

These two examples can only hint at the complex processes involved in the social organisation of caring. What they suggest, however, is that an understanding of caring requires a fundamental reassessment of both the institutions of caring (the family, the community, the state) and the conditions to which they give rise (dependency, poverty, powerlessness). In this reassessment, caring emerges not so much as an expression of women's natural feelings of compassion and connectedness, as the psychological analyses suggest, but as an expression of women's position within a particular kind of society in which the twin forces of capitalism and patriarchy are at work. Caring, it appears, describes more than the universal feelings women have: it describes the specific kind of labour they perform in our society.

In what ways does this perspective sharpen our understanding? Firstly, it suggests that caring is not simply something women do for themselves, to achieve their femininity. It is something women do for others, to keep them alive. As Margery Spring Rice's study of working-class wives documents, women care so their husbands and children can survive (Spring Rice 1981, p. 106):

Her husband *must* be fed as upon him depends the first of all necessities, money. The children must be fed. Equally husband and children must be clothed, not only fairly warmly but, for school or work, fairly decently. Naturally they suffer from the poverty of the home, the lack of sufficient food and clothes and warmth and comfort, but it is undoubtedly true that . . . the mother will be the first to do without.

The extent to which caring is a labour which ensures life, as much as an emotion which expresses love, is apparent in those relationships where the recipient of care is disabled. The 1981 EOC report describes the experiences of those who care for elderly and handicapped dependants, where 'life' is something bartered between carer and cared-for. 'It is 24-hour care. I do everything for her, wash, bake, iron, shop, cook.

It's destroyed my life absolutely. My normal life is finished'
(EOC, 1981, p. 17).

Secondly, as this study indicates, caring relationships are
not the exclusive preserve of the 'healthy' nuclear family.
Women organise and reorganise their lives to meet the needs
of parents and relatives who grow older, husbands who
become incapacitated and handicapped children who move
into adulthood.

Thirdly, as empirical studies of the elderly and handicapped
reveal, the 'daily grind' of caring cannot be defined in abstract.
What is demanded of carers is determined by the perceived
capabilities of the dependant and the provision of resources
and services outside the family. Both these in turn are shaped
by the economic and ideological climate in which the needs
of dependants and the responsibilities of carers are defined.
This climate, as we know, is currently changing rapidly, and
with it, the labour that women perform as the carers of
children and husbands, the sick, the handicapped and the
elderly (CIS, 1981).

Caring is thus experienced as an unspecific and unspeci-
fiable kind of labour, the contours of which shift constantly.
Since it aims, like so much women's work, 'to make cohesive
what is often fragmentary and disintegrating', it is only visible
when it is not done (Adams, 1971, p. 559; Graham, 1982).
As Adrienne Rich notes, caring is an unending labour characterised by 'its attention to small chores, errands, work that
others constantly undo, small children's constant needs'
(Rich, 1980, p. 43).

Fourthly, caring is not only a diffuse and unbounded form
of labour, it is also a privatised one. Although springing from
the co-operative nature of women's psyche, it is one which
typically remains unseen and unspoken. It is something
women do as an expression of their connectedness with
others, yet is something they invariably do alone. Caring, in
our society, demands the adoption of a life-style which
isolates the carer (and frequently the cared-for) from the
outside world. Home, as the setting in which most caring is
carried out, becomes not so much a haven from the rigours of
the labour market, as a prison. Again, Margery Spring Rice
captures the realities of caring (1981, pp. 105, 106):

the working mother is almost entirely cut off from contact
with the world outside her house. She eats, sleeps, 'rests'
on the scene of her labour, and her labour is entirely
solitary. . . . Whatever the emotional compensations, whatever her devotion, her family creates her labour, and
tightens the bonds that tie her to the lonely and narrow
sphere of 'home'.

Although Spring Rice describes the domestic situation of
carers, escaping into employment does not necessarily remove
'the coercion of privacy' (Dahl and Snare, 1978). A woman's
paid work is often the market equivalent of her unpaid work
at home. The growth of service-sector employment has
involved the transfer of many of the more highly specialised
aspects of caring from the home, with the result that in
secretarial and clerical work, in nursing, teaching and social
work, the woman finds again 'her self always in response to
others—an unending, unspecific task of helping, nurturing,
educating, supporting' (Garrett, 1977, p. 22). As a result,
women often confront in their roles outside the home, the
very demands which oppress them within it (Adams, 1971,
pp. 558, 559):

Both family and professional commitments incorporate
the insidious notion that the needs, demands and difficulties of other people should be women's major, if not
exclusive, concern and that meeting these must take
precedence over all other claims . . .

A conception of caring-as-women's-work clearly advances
our thinking in a number of ways. We can appreciate its
economic and ideological nature, as a labour which, although
essential for survival, is invisible, devalued and privatised.
However, in its emphasis on the structural forces at work,
such a perspective can quickly lose sight of the personal
significance of caring. Stripped of the emotional bonds which
encompass it, caring becomes redefined as 'tending', 'the
actual work of looking after those who, temporarily or
permanently, cannot do so for themselves' (Parker, 1981,
p. 17). But caring is more than this: a kind of domestic labour
performed on people. It can't be 'cleaned up' into such

categories without draining the relationship between carer and cared-for of the dimension we most need to confront. Caring cannot be understood objectively and abstractly, but only as a subjective experience in which we are all, for better or worse, involved.

Conclusion

This chapter has attempted to draw the boundaries around the concept of caring. It has been suggested that caring defines a specific type of social relationship based upon both affection and service, and, moreover, that these two interlocking transactions have been carefully dismantled by social scientists, and reconstructed within the separate disciplinary domains of psychology and social policy. In this process of reconstruction, the everyday experience of caring as a labour of love has been lost: left stranded between the scientific frameworks into which other social phenomena apparently fit so well.

The two frameworks identified in the chapter are—inevitably—crudely drawn. However, they do alert us to the nature of the empirical and theoretical material which addresses, albeit obliquely, the question of caring. Fundamental to the two perspectives is a distinction between two types of social relationship. These social relationships are defined in gender terms. One is prototypically female, and here caring, as either a psychological or material transaction, is present. In the other, 'caring' is replaced by 'doing', a concept seen to define a prototypically male relationship to the social world. From this common starting-point, the perspectives diverge: tracing the origins of the gender division to the needs of the personality system on the one hand and the socio-economic system on the other.

Both perspectives, it is argued, offer a reified picture of caring. The psychological studies tell us what caring means in emotional terms, but not in material terms. By neglecting the material basis of caring, an aspect so central to the understanding of gender relations, the psychological perspective is seen to run dangerously close to essentialism, to an argument that caring reflects women's biological nature and women's psychic needs. As Sayers observes, this perspective ends up legitimating the status quo, a status quo built around the glorification of the specific and special kinds of relations which women have with the social world (Sayers, 1982). The more recent work within social policy, particularly that initiated by marxist-feminist writers, has corrected this tendency by focusing on caring (and dependency) as a political and economic relation supported by the wider system of gender divisions. In spelling out the material benefits for the state, this work has highlighted the exploitation of women's labour on which the present organisation of family care rests. In so doing it tends to underplay the symbolic bonds that hold the caring relationship together. The roots of people's deep resistance to the socialisation of care is thus lost. Whether provided through the institutions of the state or through the intervention of 'good neighbours' in the community, both carers and their dependants recognise that the substitute services are not 'care', since they lack the very qualities of commitment and affection which transform caring-work into a life-work, a job into a duty. As Finch and Groves note, a feminist analysis which reveals the exploitative nature of the caring relationship still leaves us with the question 'would you put your sister into care?' (Finch and Groves, 1982).

Such unanswered questions are the inevitable result of a piecemeal approach to caring, in which labour and love are analysed separately. They relate, too, to a more fundamental problem. It is possible, as in other areas of the social world, that, in fragmenting the experience of caring into its two constituent parts, that its most distinctive and most compelling qualities have been lost. Although the process of retrieval has begun, there is still little empirical evidence on which to build an alternative perspective.

As a beginning, this chapter has argued that caring is experienced as a labour of love. Unlike the labour-contracts negotiated through the cash-nexus, caring is a work-role whose form and content is shaped (and continually reshaped) by our intimate social and sexual relationships. This work-role, moreover, provides the basis on which women negotiate their entrée into these intimate relationships and into the wider structures—of the community, the state and the economy--which surround them.

What this chapter argues is that the experience of caring is the medium through which women are accepted into and feel they belong in the social world. It is the medium through which they gain admittance into both the private world of the home and the public world of the labour market. It is through caring in an informal capacity--as mothers, wives, daughters, neighbours, friends--and through formal caring--as nurses, secretaries, cleaners, teachers, social workers--that women enter and occupy their place in society.

If this understanding of the experience of caring is correct, then it suggests that we must begin our analysis by recognising that caring defines both the identity and the activity of women in Western society. It defines what it feels like to be a woman in a male-dominated and capitalist social order. Men negotiate their social position through something recognised as 'doing', doings based on 'knowledge' which enables them to 'think' and to engage in 'skilled work'. Women's social position is negotiated through a different kind of activity called 'caring', a caring informed not by knowledge but by 'intuition' through which women find their way into 'unskilled' jobs. Thus, caring is not something on the periphery of our social order; it marks the point at which the relations of capital and gender intersect. It should be the place we begin, and not end our analysis of modern society. As Stacey notes (1981, p. 189):

> We shall never be able to understand the social processes going on around us so long as we tacitly or overtly deny the part played by the givers and receivers of 'care' and 'service', the victims of socialisation processes, the unpaid labourers in the processes of production and reproduction.

CHAPTER 2

Why do women care?[1]

Clare Ungerson

At first sight the title of this chapter seems rather cold, implying as it does that there is some problem about our feelings for our fellow human beings and that 'caring' is not a spontaneous emotion based, simply, on affection. But this is to make the all too easy, but mistaken, elision between caring *about* someone and caring *for* that person. These two meanings of the word 'care' are totally different, both in terms of their basis and in terms of the implications for carer and cared-for. Caring *about* someone, in the sense of feeling affection for them, is based on spontaneous feelings of affinity, and as an emotion *per se* it has little implication for how people spend their time—except that they might want to spend it together. On the other hand, caring *for* someone, in the sense of servicing their needs, may have little or nothing to do with caring *about* someone. The basis for the provision of the services of caring may be based not on affection and affinity, but on other modes of obligation: the carer may be paid for her services, or provide them because she feels generally compassionate for all people in need, or feels subject to social norms about the nature of relationships with close kin and the kinds of services socially expected of her in those particular relationships. Moreover, caring *for* someone necessarily involves the consumption of time on the part of the carer: as Roy Parker has recently put it, caring for 'comprises such things as feeding, washing, lifting, protecting, representing and comforting' (Parker, 1980, p. 3). All these tasks necessarily take time; moreover time spent in carrying out many caring tasks is primarily devoted to them and, except in the case of tasks concerned with 'listening out for' the cared for or simply 'being there', cannot be used for other non-caring purposes. In contrast, caring about someone can be experienced without using up time devoted exclusively to experiencing those emotions. Thus caring for a person, or, as Roy Parker has recently renamed it, 'tending' a person (Parker, 1980) has two important distinguishing features: firstly, it describes provision for needs where the sense of obligation on the part of the carer is socially rather than affectively constructed, through payment for services rendered or the exigencies of a social norm. Secondly, the practice of 'tending' consumes time, often—though not always—in such a way that the carer is unable to combine tending with other time-consuming activities and may even become too exhausted to use her remaining time as she might otherwise wish.

Thus, in order to convey the sense of 'caring for' as socially constructed and time consuming the question in this chapter's title should really be altered to 'Why do women tend?'. This raises two further questions: firstly, why is it that women rather than men tend—in other words, what is it about the social construction of caring that means that women predominate as carers rather than men? Secondly, while women predominantly carry out these tasks presently, will they continue to do so given changes in their material circumstances and the consumption of their time in other tasks such as—and particularly—paid work? In this chapter it is the second question rather than the first that will be addressed, since in her discussion of caring that women do to demonstrate their femininity, Hilary Graham (see Chapter 1 in this volume) discusses the ideology of caring and its relationship with sex and gender. In order to ask whether women will continue to find time to care I shall discuss the interaction of sex role stereotyping and women's material circumstances at two interfaces—the labour market and the state. In other words, I shall attempt to indicate what are the ideological and material determinants of how women spend their time at home and in paid work as those determinants are mediated by the labour market and social policies, and whether those determinants are likely to change in the foreseeable future. But this discussion has a major caveat: many of the issues I shall raise do not, as yet, have answers derived from empirical research —although the data presented in other chapters in this volume provide a rich vein for further delving. The bare fact is that recognition by social scientists that tending devolves primarily on women, and that there are important social, economic, and sociological implications of this, has arrived remarkably slowly (Stacey, 1981) and women's role in tending has only very recently started to be unravelled by the more pioneering (Land, 1978; Wilkin, 1979; Finch and Groves, 1980). As a result we tend to be left with more questions than answers, and many answers tend to be based on little more than educated speculation.

One striking example of our ignorance is that while we now know a considerable amount about the actual distribution of time spent on tending by husbands and wives, both when caring for young and normal children, and for older dependent relatives (Wilkin, 1979; Derow, 1981; Nissel and Bonnerjea, 1982), we know almost nothing about how and why this allocation of time occurs. All these studies show that wives and mothers spend a great deal more time on tending than their husbands, irrespective of whether the wives are working for pay or not, but we remain ignorant as to the basis of this consistent, and apparently universal, outcome. Is this allocation of time and distribution of tasks the result of explicit and implicit decisions made within families between husbands and wives, parents and children, brothers and sisters, boys and girls, carers and cared for? And on what basis are these decisions being made? Do they derive from the power of men over women in the domestic arena and/or the labour market, or do they reflect the wishes of women carers themselves, or the needs and demands of the cared-for, or the assumptions about sex roles embedded in social policies, or the ideology of sex role stereotyping and prevailing ideas of women's 'proper' place? I am not going to answer these questions, let alone attempt to weigh the power of the different forces mentioned above: the following paragraphs amount to the 'educated speculation' referred to earlier, omit the question of relations within families not because it is unimportant but because we know so little about it, and are restricted to discussion of the labour market and the state.

The Labour Market

Commentators on women as paid workers and women as housewives have been saying for a very long time that women have 'two roles' (Myrdal and Klein, 1956). Moreover, feminist sociologists and economists have more recently shown how women's role in reproduction has a profound effect on their role in production and *vice versa* (see Pollert, 1981). The tensions for women between paid work and unpaid domestic labour can, at an individualistic level, be described in terms of 'opportunity costs'—that is, if women 'choose' to spend their time in paid work then one of the perceived costs of doing so is loss of time to carry out domestic tasks at home; similarly if women 'choose' to spend their time at home then the perceived costs consist of actual loss of earnings and possible companionship at work. This concept of 'opportunity costs', while it does give a false impression that everyone has 'opportunities' and merely sets about maximising their satisfactions, is a very useful one for our purposes because it can be used to encapsulate individual decision making about how, why, and when to consume time in particular ways.

Women in Britain have apparently worked their way through the minefield of 'opportunity costs' by taking on part-time work in unusually large numbers—compared to the rest of the developed capitalist world. Between 1961 and 1978, the number of women working rose from 7.5 million to 9.5 million, and almost all this increase has been due to the entry into the labour market of part-timers—indeed, during that same period the proportion of full-time women workers actually fell by 2 per cent (Elias, 1980a). At the same time the actual number of hours worked by mothers (for whom the data is generally available) stayed steady or declined slightly (Moss, 1980). Economists suggest that married women's behaviour in the labour market is problematic: while it is clear that women enter the labour market in response to increases in available wages, the actual number of hours that women work once they have taken jobs appear to bear very little relation either to the wages they themselves or their husbands earn (Layard *et al.*, 1980). Economists have some difficulty in explaining these incongruent kinds of result because they tend to build models of human behaviour that assume a 'rationality' based exclusively on material, or monetary, factors. But, as far as women are concerned, such material explanations cannot take into account the ideological structure that women face—which indicates that their responsibilities are primarily domestic.

The point is that women appear to be entering the labour market in order to gain a reasonable income for themselves (Pahl, 1980) and a better material standard of living for their families (Marsh, 1979), but the limit to the *hours* they actually work is imposed by a set of beliefs that they have about what they really *ought* to be doing for the good of their families back home. Thus I will suggest the important determinants of how women spend their time are twofold: firstly, material conditions, both at home and in the labour market, and, secondly, the ideology of women's 'place' as internalised by themselves, their husbands and their dependants at home, and their bosses—of whom the most powerful are almost always male—at work. It is the interaction between these two sets of forces that ultimately determine how women perceive the 'opportunity costs' of working at home or in the labour market.

Of the two sets of forces, material conditions appear to change much more rapidly than ideology. As Michele Barrett has argued, there is no material reason why women are expected to carry out certain tasks in and beyond the home and men are expected to carry out a different set. She suggests that ideology is of prime importance, and that that ideology has its material base in the past (Barrett, 1980). Material conditions, on the other hand, seem to change much more quickly: the rapid growth of women in the labour market over the past twenty years is one example; the changing relativities between men's and women's earnings are another. (Elias has estimated that between 1968 and 1975, net real earnings of women grew by 25-30 per cent compared with only 9-16 per cent for their husbands (Elias, 1980a); in contrast, during the recent recession women's wage rates appear to have fallen away faster than men's (*The Times*, 11 June 1981).) Thus, when it comes to forecasting the future one can with some safety predict the ideological environment within which men and women work out their roles, but with far less safety suggest what material conditions are likely to be, or what the impact of those changing conditions are likely to be on women's work.

Clearly Britain's economy is going through a sea-change at the moment; mass unemployment of men and women, a very rapid decline of manufacturing, and the projected mass introduction of micro-technology particularly in the service sector are the three most important features. Hence it is peculiarly problematic to say anything at the moment about the future of 'women's work', women's wage rates in relation to men's, and the ensuing changes in opportunity costs for women staying at home. Nevertheless, despite all these rapid and unpredictable changes it is clear that women's wage rates and their position in the occupational hierarchy owe a great deal to the ideology that male bosses carry around in their heads about what women's commitment to home and work *ought* to be. In 1975, Audrey Hunt reported on the OPCS survey on *Management Attitudes and Practices towards Women at Work* (Hunt, 1975). This survey of the 'formulators' and 'implementors' of personnel policy at 223 large firms (over 100 employees) in Britain carried out in 1973 talked almost exclusively to men in high managerial positions. Relatively low proportions of their own wives were working, and Table 2.1 indicates how little these husbands themselves did around the house. The ten married women in the sample had a very jaundiced view of their own husband's lack of help. All of them said their husbands gave *no* help with child care and hardly any of their husbands helped with other household tasks apart from decorating and gardening. Sex role stereotyping extended into the managers' aspirations for their children's education; many more boys were expected to go to university than girls, and large proportions of girls were expected to become nurses, teachers and secretaries (Hunt, 1975, p. 40). The rest of Hunt's report is taken up with investigating these managers' attitudes to the employment and promotion of men and women workers in their firms, and it is quite clear that ideas about their home lives spilt over into their views of women at work. On the whole, the managers thought men were considerably better at not taking days off for sickness and other reasons and were far more

Table 2.1 *Tasks done around house by married men* (%)

| | Proportion of task done by husbands | | | | | |
	None	One quarter	About one half	More than one half	All	Not stated
Formulators						
Preparing, cooking meals	52.4	38.4	6.3	0.2	—	2.7
Washing up	27.8	53.1	11.0	1.8	3.3	3.0
Washing, ironing, mending	85.2	11.0	0.4	0.2	—	3.3
Other housework	57.7	32.1	6.7	0.2	—	3.3
Care of children	52.8	35.0	8.7	0.6	—	3.9
Shopping, errands	40.7	34.8	16.7	1.8	0.2	5.8
Household decorations, repairs	24.0	13.0	11.8	16.3	31.3	3.6
Gardening	11.0	8.1	25.4	16.7	35.2	3.6
Other tasks	83.9	4.5	0.4	—	4.1	7.1
Proportion of all tasks	1.4	73.8	17.1	—	—	7.7
Implementors						
Preparing, cooking meals	58.3	32.5	6.8	0.2	0.4	1.8
Washing up	25.2	46.3	17.6	2.6	6.8	1.5
Washing, ironing, mending	85.8	11.8	0.6	0.2	—	1.5
Other housework	56.0	28.9	13.2	0.2	—	1.8
Care of children	67.4	26.3	4.4	0.6	—	1.3
Shopping, errands	35.8	29.9	25.0	5.2	0.2	3.9
Household decorations, repairs	22.2	10.3	16.2	11.4	37.4	2.5
Gardening	9.1	8.3	21.9	15.5	42.7	2.5
Other tasks	89.7	1.4	—	—	4.4	4.5
Proportion of all tasks	1.5	72.1	18.7	1.1	—	6.6

Source: Audrey Hunt, 1975, p.38.

likely to stay with one firm whereas they thought women worked harder and more conscientiously (ibid., p. 94). It turned out, when Audrey Hunt looked at the facts, that women were not that much more likely to take time off to deal with their families. Clearly, such a view of women's lowered commitment to their work will have an effect on their recruitment and promotion prospects, although other factors are no doubt just as important. For example, 47 per cent of the managers thought men more intelligent than women and 55 per cent thought men had more pleasant personalities (ibid., p. 81). The point is that if male managers continue to carry around an idea of women's 'proper' place at home, which is reflected in and reflects the organisation of their own home lives, then it is extremely unlikely that women's wages and promotion prospects will alter a great deal, if at all. In other words, the opportunity costs for women to stay at home are almost certain to continue to be lower than men's; hence, if there is a need for someone to be looked after at home, *it makes sense in material terms and will continue to make sense for the wife to give up her job or reduce her working hours. Thus the ideology of housework and woman's place within it has a material impact on women's paid work which in turn serves to reinforce that very ideology*.

This is not to deny that the loss of women's earnings is important to caring families. In Muriel Nissel and Lucy Bonnerjea's survey of twenty-two married couples caring for a dependent relative fifteen of the wives were not working at all, and of those nine had given up work specifically because of the need to care for their dependent relative (Nissel and Bonnerjea, 1982, p. 51). Table 2.2 reproduces data from Nissel and Bonnerjea and refers to the ten wives from their sample who wanted eventually to return to work. For comparative purposes, and in order to develop further the point about it being more 'rational' for women than men to give up work to care for someone, given current sexist practices at work, I have added the average earnings of men in more or less equivalent jobs, and additional data on the earnings of the husbands of these particular wives. It is clear from the table that all these women had given up considerable financial independence particularly if they had been working full-time.

Table 2.2 *Previous occupations and potential earnings of wives who said they would like to take up a job again; their husbands' earnings*[a]*; average earnings of men in approximately equivalent jobs*[b]

	Average gross weekly earnings (£ per week)		
Wives' occupation	Wives	Their husbands	Men in jobs equivalent to wives
Shop assistant	54,7	111	90.3
Soft-toy maker	61.3	157	94.7 (footwear worker)
Sales supervisor	72.7	117.5	112.2
Driver	80.0	110	103.5
Secretary	80.2	128	96.3 (general clerk)
Secretary	80.2	97	
Welfare officer	99.1	150	124.8
Primary school teacher	106.7	117	123.5
Occupational therapist	107.9	180	125.8
Postgraduate research	128.0	300	154.4

a Data on husbands' earnings kindly supplied by Muriel Nissel in a personal communication.
b Data on wives' potential earnings and earnings of men in equivalent jobs taken from *New Earnings Survey*, Table 86, Part D (DE, January 1981). This gives earnings for April 1980, the date nearest to the date of the Nissel and Bonnerjea survey (Nissel and Bonnerjea, 1982, p. 51).

Moreover, there is no doubt, both from this study and from Lynne Hamill's on *Wives as Sole and Joint Breadwinners* (Hamill, 1978) that their contribution to the family income has been very important. But as is also clear from the table, the opportunity costs are less when women give up their jobs than when men do. And for these particular households, unsurprisingly, all the wives earned rather less than their husbands.

Thus the sexist structure of the labour market imposes its own *diktat* on the structure and organisation of family life. And, in its turn, the structure and organisation of family life, with the man as 'chief breadwinner' and the woman as housewife, mother, general factotum and low-waged part-time worker, reduces the possibility of detaching the labour market from sexist practice; the position of women within the family is a great gain to men as husbands and men as bosses. But, as I suggested earlier, the British economy is currently going through a sea-change, of which one of the features is mass unemployment of both men and women. Most predictions point to a growth of unemployment, possibly to 4 million workers by the mid-1980s levelling off to a possible steady state of 3 million which will last for a considerable length of time. The effects of such widespread unemployment on family life will be important and are, in many ways, unpredictable since a similar nationwide experience last occurred in the 1930s when a great many other features of British economic and social life were rather different. But obviously one of the effects will be that the structure of the labour market will no longer determine the structure of family life in quite the way that it does at the moment, since for many families the labour market will be an irrelevancy. There simply won't be any work for millions of men, women, and their school-leaving children. In other words, the opportunity costs for many men and women to stay at home will be reduced to zero, or even, depending on the interaction of supplementary benefit and taxation on the one hand, and wage rates and transport costs on the other, attain a negative value. Under these circumstances the ideology of women's 'place' and material circumstances cease to reinforce each other, and the opportunity arises to develop concrete practices which run counter to prevailing ideology. In short, where married men are unemployed and there are no local vacancies it *may* be the case that men will be more willing to take on the 'caring' role. Some recent research indicates that this is doubtful: in a small study of the impact of the introduction of 'flexitime' on the division of labour at home, Lee found that men's contribution to household work did not increase significantly except that they spent more time maintaining the car and in 'child socialisation activities'. In other words, most fathers took the opportunity to amplify their 'masculine' role (the exceptions were those of a 'radical' orientation) (Lee, 1981). But despite the fact that flexitime and unemployment have the same zero opportunity cost for time spent in 'caring', they may be rather different in their impact on conjugal roles. Paid work, after all, is the central feature of mid to late twentieth-century constructions of 'masculinity'; the absence of available paid work for men might therefore undermine other aspects of the social construction of the male gender; or it might lead to the amplification of other 'masculine' traits, such as dominance at home. It is also important to bear in mind that caring for normal children may have a rather different ideological construction from caring for other dependants, such as spouses or elderly confused parents, and that the impact of unemployment on caring under these circumstances may be rather different. It is clear, however, that we know very little about different kinds of tending and the differential impact of changing material circumstances. While research in this area would be both difficult and sensitive, it would be useful and interesting to discover how long-term unemployment alters conjugal roles as far as caring is concerned. Such research could, *ceteris paribus*, begin to unpack the twin gorgons of 'ideology' and material circumstances, since the latter would no longer be particularly relevant; the impact of prevailing ideology on conjugal role-playing would hence be more clearly illuminated.

State intervention

But, of course, all other things are *not* equal. The state intervenes in the domestic division of labour both at an ideological and at a material level, and at no point does that intervention become stronger than when the 'male breadwinner' is unemployed. It is then that the earnings rule (applicable to wives and currently based on a mere £17 per week) comes into operation thus pushing the wife into dependence on her husband. Much of this state intervention in family life operates through the medium of social security benefits and has been pioneeringly analysed by Hilary Land (see Land, 1978); analysis of the particular case of the invalid care allowance has been similarly dissected by Dulcie Groves and Janet Finch (Chapter 8 in this volume). In all cases, the message comes through loud and clear; as Hilary Land has put it: 'The social security system ignores the fact that most families are dependent on *two* earners; it actively discourages role reversal and it encourages women to give priority to their responsibilities in the home' (Land, 1978, p. 262). The critique of these policies that these authors present is largely concerned with four aspects. Firstly, they argue the policies are based on 'myths' and do not reflect the reality of family life in late twentieth-century Britain; secondly, the policies contain considerable disincentives to women to work and thereby combine with other factors in the labour market to depress women's wages; thirdly, they fail to compensate women for loss of earnings although they do compensate men (e.g. the invalid care allowance); and fourthly, they play a central part in maintaining an ideology of the nature of family life and the particular roles within families that men and women should play:

> The fact that certain values favouring the interests of men rather than women have been embodied in a variety of social policies over a long period of time, both formally in the legislation and by the way in which they are allocated or used, indicates that social policies are a very important means by which these values, and hence major inequalities between the sexes, are maintained (Land 1978, p. 284).

There are two interesting questions here which, so far, have not been tackled in this literature. Both questions are concerned with the impact of this legislation and allocation of resources on the actual *behaviour* of men and women when it comes to caring and approaching the labour market. The first question concerns the impact of the ideology fostered by social policies, while the second concerns the impact of the structure of state benefits and resources on the way men and women actually behave.

The operation of ideology about women's domestic place is complicated, interacts with material conditions, and as far as women are concerned may be changing, although men's views are probably changing far more slowly if at all (Marsh, 1979). The fact that the state consistently pursues a chimera of family life, but a chimera which nevertheless accords with people's view of what family life *ought* to be like, *may* be important in maintaining this ideology and hence, possibly, determine behaviour. The difficulty, of course, lies in isolating purely ideological effects and the role of different social institutions in promoting them. There is no doubt that we are all, *in some way*, affected. State intervention in our domestic lives is a universal experience: as taxpayers, recipients of and contributors to national insurance, users of the NHS and state education. Does the impact of the state view of how we ought to relate to each other within our families persuade us to behave in that manner, or does it depress, annoy and even provoke rebellion? There is some evidence that far from promoting and maintaining the ideology of the 'normal' family the actual practice of allocating supplementary benefit, for example, enrages the recipients. A study of single mothers on supplementary benefit by Jane Streather and Stuart Weir (Streather and Weir, 1974) is replete with examples of mothers made angry and upset by pressure to name the 'liable relative'—i.e. the father of their children—and to go to court for maintenance orders. These mothers were angry enough to take matters further through the Citizen's Rights Office of CPAG and hence we must assume that their self-selection implies atypicality. Other more generalisable studies, particularly of women in receipt of peri-natal care, have indicated that a common response to the ideology of the subordination of women perpetuated in maternity wards is depression and alienation, rather than sheer anger (Oakley, 1980). But a major strand in the development of the women's movement, both here and in the United States, has been the growth of self-help health care women's groups based on a critique (often an angry one) of male-dominated techniques of medical intervention (Boston Women's Health Book Collective, 1971). Much of this critique is concerned with the relationships between male doctors and their women patients, rather than assumptions made by these medical men about relations between husbands and wives. It is clear, however, from other studies—particularly that by P. M. Strong—that assumptions are made in hospital about the particular role of mothers and fathers, although the response of parents tends to be an accepting rather than an angry one:

> When a couple did attend a clinic together, staff placed fathers in a subordinate position to their spouses. Questions were asked directly to the mothers and, though fathers sometimes added their own comments to which staff

might reply, they normally returned to the mother for their next question . . . fathers who had a lot to say had usually to interrupt a running conversation. The structure of the situation automatically defined them as rude and inconsiderate: a fact which such fathers usually acknowledged with grins and apologies (Strong, 1979, pp. 61–2).

I am suggesting, then, that responses to state intervention and its ideology are complicated, and under-researched. While state intervention in family life is wholly consistent and ideologically based, there is not necessarily a simple link between the existence of that particular set of assumptions and the perpetuation of that ideology in recipients' minds. Indeed, the 'ideal' family life that the state presents to the world is so rapidly becoming a minor form of family structure that it would be very surprising if more and more people, particularly women, were not made aware of the contradictory positions which the state imposes upon them. According to the state, a 'normal' woman has a husband, and is primarily housewife *and* mother. If she hasn't got a man, then she isn't 'normal' and cannot be either a housewife or a mother. Thus, where there is a male 'breadwinner' or 'liable relative' mothers are expected to be dependent on them to the extent of losing their own and their children's benefits, and are not expected to work. However, as soon as it is accepted by the state—in the form of the SBC—that there isn't a 'liable relative' then the same mothers are pressured into going to work, irrespective of the care arrangements for their children (Streather and Weir, 1974). Similarly a consistent view of the nature of femininity leads to contradictory treatment of women in different 'sick' roles. According to Oakley doctors tend to treat women with gynaecological and peri-natal problems like naughty children, but once they become mothers they are treated (according to Strong, 1979, pp. 61–2) like madonnas. Many of these contradictions are not, of course, new; but the major changes in the position of women in the twentieth century, including the enormous reduction of final family size, the compression of childbearing and rearing into a very few years of a woman's adult life, the expansion of female paid labour, the acceleration of divorce rates, and the growth of single parenting, have all rendered the nature of state intervention increasingly mythological and contradictory.

It may be the case that the state's view of our lives does colour our own view. Paradoxically and somewhat ironically, Julian Fulbrook, in a study of appellants' views of supplementary benefit tribunals had the following small insight:

> One substantial cause of benefit fraud cases must surely be the simple inability of claimants to comprehend the regulations. Two cases involving non-disclosure of a wife's earnings in this survey clearly arose largely from the husband's confusion. Another facet to these cases was that the husband clearly believed in the common working-class view that wives go out to work for their own 'pin-money' and not for the household budget (Fulbrook, 1975, p. 13).

According to this evidence the state's view 'works', though in a counter-productive manner. But such evidence is slim to say the least and I think we need to test Hilary Land's conclusion that 'social policies are a very important means by which these values, and hence major inequalities between the sexes, are maintained'. In my view, this conclusion has the status of a hypothesis; the range of response to consistent state intervention, increasingly contradictory and contorted as it is, lies between submission on the one hand and rebellion on the other.

Of course, research into the impact of ideology on people's lives inevitably leads to questions about how ideology and behaviour interact, and I have already suggested that this is very problematic, particularly as behaviour is subject to such a range of determinants and constraints. But the second question I have outlined, about the way in which the structure of state benefits and the allocation of state resources actually determines the way people behave, more directly tackles the issue of material effects. The point is that we know very little about how the invalid care allowance, the attendance allowance, the allocation of home helps, day hospital places and aids for the disabled etc. actually *work* in economic terms. It may, of course, be the case that take-up of the cash benefits is so low and the allocation of services so restricted that they can only be said to have a neutral effect. In a small-scale study of 111 caring households, the Equal Opportunities Commission found that only very small minorities received a wide range of benefits and services (EOC, 1980).

Table 2.3 *Household: by type of help received*

Type of help	Number receiving	Percentage receiving
Attendance allowance	17	15
Mobility allowance	10	9
Invalidity pension	7	6
Other/just social security	9	8
Rent rebate	8	7
TV allowance	3	3
Clothes allowance	3	3
Heating allowance	3	3
Special food allowance	2	2
Car allowance	2	2
Home help (free)	16	14
Meals on wheels regularly	3	3
Meals on wheels sometimes/on waiting list	3	3
Day centre visits	10	9
Old peoples club visits	10	9

(Total all households 111) Source: EOC, 1980.

But assuming that many caring families do receive some form of aid, what is their effect on the economic behaviour of women? Do they, by lowering the opportunity costs of staying at home through the attendance allowances, provide incentives for women to stay at home and care for their dependants? Or do they, by assuming that married women are primarily housewives rather than workers, actually push married women into the labour market because they withhold certain benefits such as the invalid care allowance and resources such as home helps and day hospitals on the grounds that such women can 'cope' unaided—thereby reducing their total resources relative to other families? If research into these questions were developed, it may well turn out, as research into the impact of, for example, the cohabitation and the earnings rules has indicated that much of state legislation is counter-productive. In the case of the cohabitation rule it can break up rather than foster embryonic nuclear families; in the case of the earnings rule, which is designed to maintain work incentives, it can push women out of work altogether or into the informal economy. Similarly, the allocation of resources to carers on the basis not of their 'needs' but according to their expected ability to 'cope' may well reduce the time that the so-called 'copers' are able and willing to spend on caring, since they may prefer to generate additional resources for themselves and their dependants in the labour market. On the other hand, it may place them in such straitened circumstances that the quality of their care is seriously and consistently reduced.

The final form of state intervention in domestic lives that has implications for the way in which women spend their time is the allocation of social services; home helps, day hospital places, advice about cash benefits, and aids for the disabled which enable them to play a greater part in their own care or reduce the time taken by others in tending tasks, are all important sources of help for the carer and may enable her or him to spend time at work. We do have some evidence that some social services are allocated partially on the basis of assumptions about sex roles. For example, home helps are more likely to be allocated to men living alone than women living alone (Hunt, 1970, p. 238) and there is some evidence that those with sons rather than daughters are more likely to get home help (Hunt, 1970, p. 178). The central 'gatekeeper' who largely determines initial access to such services is the general practitioner (Hunt, 1970, p. 201) and yet we have very little direct knowledge about their assumptions concerning sex roles and the duties, responsibilities and abilities of the carers, be they female or male. The relationship between carer and doctor is a complicated one, and it is clearly not simply a case of doctors deciding that women can drop everything and 'cope' whereas men can't. The carers, too, play an active part in the allocation of these services and, as Hilary Graham argues (Chapter 1 in this volume), they may well have accepted their caring role as inevitable and unaidable. Nevertheless in the EOC survey of carers, the authors argued that: 'it was also clear that if there were a woman in the house, a request for a home help was likely to be refused. "We cannot have a home help because I am at home"' (EOC, 1980, p. 36). But it remains unclear to me whether this was the carer's own view of her situation and her responsibilities or the reason she had been given for refusing her the service. Lucy Bonnerjea's analysis of the relationship between carers and doctors gets, I think, nearer to reality.

> *Women had to define the situation as a crisis to themselves* (my emphasis); then they had to present an acceptable definition of a breakdown to the doctor; then help would be provided. One interviewee offered some advice to others in her position: 'You have to be a damn good actress; if you're seen to be coping, then you're left alone and there's no help, no share of responsibility. It's very unfair' (Nissel and Bonnerjea, 1981, p. 20).

Research in this area is difficult but there is already a considerable body of literature that analyses conversations between professionals and clients or patients (Byrne and Long, 1976; Strong, 1979; Oakley, 1980. Baldock and Prior, 1981). Such research could and should be repeated, with a view to establishing the nature of the 'gatekeeping' relationship between doctors and carers; of particular interest would be the doctors' treatment of the legitimacy or otherwise of how women spend their time outside the home.

Conclusions

From this brief survey of the possible range of answers to the question 'Why do women care?' one thing is evident, another unclear. It is, firstly, quite obvious that research is only just beginning to scratch the surface. We know a little about women's attitudes towards their own domestic role (Oakley, 1974; Marsh, 1979) but very little indeed about how women, under particular circumstances, interpret their role to respond to those circumstances. We can guess at some of the costs and benefits for individual women of paid and unpaid labour and speculate about the future relationship between work at home and work in the labour market, but we know very little about how husbands and wives work out these economic relationships within the family. We can talk generally about 'caring' and women's role within it; but much of the existing discussion of caring by women is largely restricted to the tending of normal children (e.g. Oakley, 1974; Moss and Fonda, 1980; Lee, 1981), and we need to distinguish at least two further categories of tending: first that of caring for husbands, and second, caring for other dependent relatives who are, for different reasons, unable to look after themselves. We may find, with a more sophisticated taxonomy of tending, that the ideology of 'women's place' has different impacts under different tending circumstances—for example, it may be that the calls on a woman's time by her own small child and the assumptions that social institutions make about mothers and children are of a different order from the calls of the same woman's elderly mother, or ailing husband. Thus this much is clear: we need more research.

But, secondly, I have tried to argue—with less certainty— that we can speculate that women rather than men predominate amongst informal carers because there are powerful material and ideological forces that determine that they will so do. Moreover, I have suggested that as far as the labour market is concerned, those material forces will continue because the discrepancies between men's and women's earnings show no sign of abating and reflect employers' own views of women's 'proper' place—and these are unlikely to alter quickly. The state, I have suggested, uses particular social policies to reinforce these ideas about sex roles, but it is here that the seeds of change may lie. For the state's view of the family and roles within it is becoming more and more incongruent with the family as women and men actually experience it. This contradiction, combined with the impact on family life of mass unemployment for men as well as women, may eventually undermine the strength of sex role stereotyping. In that case, the vital tasks of tending may no longer be predominantly women's territory: but such an outcome would depend on the political power of women, at home, at the work place, and in the polity.

PART 2

The experience of caring

CHAPTER 3

Employment, women and their disabled children

Sally Baldwin and Caroline Glendinning

A number of studies have documented the extent to which, as with any dependent child, responsibility for the day-to-day care of a severely disabled child tends to fall largely and unremittingly on her/his mother (Wilkin, 1979; Glendinning, forthcoming). This chapter describes some of the ways in which the care of a child who is severely physically or mentally disabled affects women's participation in the paid labour market, and outlines the social and financial consequences of those effects for the women concerned and their families. Each topic is illustrated by findings from two empirical studies: an in-depth, longitudinal study of the parents of seventeen severely disabled children (Glendinning, forthcoming); and a large-scale survey of the incomes and expenditure patterns of 480 families with a disabled child, compared with those of a matched control group of 682 families drawn from the 1978 Family Expenditure Survey (FES) (Baldwin, 1981). The in-depth study was carried out during an evaluation of the Family Fund and related research into the needs of families with disabled children, sponsored by the Joseph Rowntree Memorial Trust.[1] The comparative study formed part of a continuation of that research programme, now funded by the Department of Health and Social Security. The children in both studies were drawn from the families who had been helped by the Family Fund and hence met the Fund's criteria of very severe disability (Bradshaw, 1980, pp. 108–9). The statistical material in this chapter is drawn from the comparative study, while the qualitative data come mainly from the longitudinal study.

Children and patterns of dependency

Severe disability in a child almost invariably increases the amount of physical, mental and emotional effort which has to be put into the day-to-day work of parenting. Table 3.1

Table 3.1 *Dependency in self-care—severely disabled children over 5 in the comparative income and expenditure study*

	No help needed %	Some help needed %	A lot of help needed %
Washing/bathing	6.4	13.0	80.6
Dressing	9.7	21.1	69.3
Feeding	22.4	48.5	29.1
Toileting	14.4	55.4	29.6*
Moving around indoors	57.3	24.7	14.4*

Total number of children over 5 = 361
*These figures do not add up to 100 per cent because of non-response.

shows the proportion of disabled children over 5 in the comparative study who were dependent on others for basic self-care. Of these children 87.5 per cent were unable to be left alone during the day for as long as a non-disabled child; 50.1 per cent could not be left alone for as long as ten minutes:

> 'She's got to be entertained all the time. She's demanding attention every minute of the day . . . and if she's not wanting attention you can guarantee she's doing something pretty evil, up to her elbows in mud or eating the privet hedge' (mother of 8-year-old mentally handicapped girl).

Forty-five per cent of parents in the comparative study were awakened several times a night three or more nights a week, to look after the disabled child; 19 per cent were up several times *every* night:

> 'She always has a broken night. Ever since she's been born . . . I've never known what it is to have a night's sleep' (mother of 9-year-old girl with spina bifida).

The extra work involved in caring for a severely disabled child is characteristic of Bayley's notion of the 'daily grind' (Bayley, 1973, ch. 15)--a wearing, routine servicing of basic functions, with no prospect of any diminution of the work involved. Oakley's distinction between the activities of housework and child-rearing is also illuminating. She characterises child-rearing as a task which is both creative and self-limiting, in contrast to housework, which is neither:

> The servicing function is basic to housework; children are people. Child-care is 'productive'; housework is not. Housework has short-term and repetitive goals; the house is cleaned today and again tomorrow and so on . . . for . . . twenty years ahead. Motherhood has a single, long-term goal, which can be described as the mother's own eventual unemployment. A 'successful' mother brings up her children to do without her (Oakley, 1974, pp. 166–7).

Obviously the care of any child involves some elements of routine 'servicing'. However caring for a severely disabled, very dependent child often has more in common with the repetitive routines of housework and less with the more creative aspects of child care than usual. Severe disablement in a child typically prolongs the duration of dependencies, normal in infancy and early childhood, long beyond their appropriate chronological ages. Developmental 'milestones' may be delayed, or never attained at all. As a result there may be much less prospect of the child's eventual transition to independence. Additionally, there may be fewer obvious rewards for parents' efforts in stimulating and nurturing children whose progress is imperceptible or whose condition is one of inevitable deterioration:

> 'They progress in spasms . . . It's terribly depressing when you get the same gibberish every day, not even a new sound. You don't want words, you just want a new sound and you don't get anything for weeks and you begin to think "Is all this teaching worth it?"' (mother of 2-year-old deaf boy).

In addition to their chronic dependency many severely disabled children are also frequently ill. Forty-two per cent

of the children in the comparative study were said not to
have good health; 47 per cent spent more time away from
school because of illness than would be expected for a child
of that age:

> 'She can be as fit as a fiddle today and then in the night
> she'll shout to me and be really poorly. You never know,
> you've got to be on edge all the while in case she does take
> poorly' (mother of 14-year-old girl with spina bifida).

Finally, attendance at hospitals and clinics, with the conse-
quent demands on parental time, is very frequent. Forty-two
per cent of children had been hospital in-patients in the year
preceding the comparative study, 19 per cent of them more
than once. Eighty-three per cent had regular out-patient
appointments: for 40 per cent these took place at more than
one location.

It would be wrong, however, to overlook the fact that the
care of a dependent child has its own compensations, and
that many women with severely disabled children derive
substantial rewards from this specialised task. These pleasures
and satisfactions, rooted in feelings of love and protectiveness,
are reinforced by 'public opinion', and by the ideological
values attached to motherhood and the family by contemporary social welfare institutions and practices.

The dominant picture is that child care is a private, family,
and typically maternal, responsibility. Virtually all women
with dependent children experience some degree of difficulty
in combining child care responsibilities with paid employment
outside the home. Mothers who want or need to take paid
work outside the home tend, therefore, to experience tensions
between their own desires to work and their 'duties' towards
their families. These difficulties and tensions will generally be
greatest when children are young and at their most dependent,
and this is reflected in the smaller proportions of women
with very young children who have paid jobs. As children
grow older, women generally move back into the labour
market in increasing numbers and for longer hours of work
(Moss, 1980).

Women whose children have severe disabilities face the
same problems as other mothers in entering the labour

market. However their child's disability substantially increases the commonplace problems and tensions of combining the roles of parent and wage-earner. As we will show, the intensification and extension of the normal burdens of infancy in effect restrict the employment opportunities and experiences of most women with severely disabled children to those typically experienced by the mothers of very young children —but with considerably reduced changes of an eventual improvement in employment prospects, conditions or wages.

However, it would be misleading to imply that women with disabled children are a homogeneous group with uniform attitudes to employment outside the home, or to the parenting tasks involved in bringing up children with severe disabilities. Not all women with a disabled child will want, or feel free, to work; not all those who want to go out to work will be able to find suitable employment or care for the child. This diversity of needs and preferences has obvious implications for policy, and these are considered in the concluding section of this chapter. First though, we look in detail at women's account of the constraints which their child's disability imposes on their opportunities to go out to work and then, using comparative data, examine the effect of these constraints on women's labour-force participation, hours and earnings.

The restrictions on employment outside the home

Why specifically are the mothers of disabled children restricted in obtaining and keeping employment outside the home? Predominant among the reasons is the sheer amount of work that can be involved in the 'daily grind' of care and which is either too demanding to leave energy for work outside the home or means that alternative care is difficult to find:

> 'First of all, in the morning Michael's got to be got up and dressed and fed and toileted, and you know he's got to be *held* on the toilet—you can't leave him. It's a couple of hours, really. And you can't do anything else while you're feeding him. If you turn round, it's spat out. It's a couple of hours getting him ready for school. And then when he comes home at half past three your time is devoted to him.

Someone has to be there. And when he goes to bed you're constantly turning him. He has to be turned so many times before he goes to sleep. And he can be sick three times in the night . . .' (mother of a 15-year-old, quadriplegic spastic boy).

Not surprisingly this boy's mother felt that she needed the time when he was at school to organise things for herself and the rest of the family, though she had at one time been a well-paid clerical worker.

School holidays can be a particular problem if mothers feel unable to rely on others (even older siblings) to look after their disabled child:

'I keep getting little jobs and then it came to the big school holiday and I had to pack it in, like I had to this year. It's hard to get a job, there's only school dinners really where you can have school holidays' (mother of 14-year-old girl with cerebral palsy).

'And then there's the school holidays. If he was all right I could always pay someone to look after him for a few hours, but no one's going to look after him now, you can't blame them really, with all the lifting and everything' (mother of 12-year-old boy with muscular dystrophy).

Frequent bouts of illness or regular hospital appointments also limit mothers' employment opportunities, if the care of the child at these times is regarded as their responsibility:

'Every so often I have to go to the hospital with him, and then when the school doctors come they like the parents to be there. I don't think [employers] would stand for so much break in time' (mother of 12-year-old boy with muscular dystrophy).

'I couldn't take a job, because you don't know when he's going to be brought home from school ill, and he's not at school every day. You couldn't take a full-time job, and I wouldn't leave him with strangers' (mother of 7-year-old boy with cystic fibrosis).

Sensitivity to the needs of their disabled child also restricts mothers' employment:

'I had a job [as a barmaid] until one night Michelle said to me "I don't want you to go to work mam". . . . I said to her "We should have a bit more money, Michelle" and she said "Don't go", so I didn't and I've never bothered going back. You don't know what goes through a child's mind . . . to tell you the truth, as she grows older she doesn't like me to leave her' (woman whose 14-year-old daughter had spina bifida).

Mothers who are able to work outside the home may, for similar reasons, experience restrictions: in the type of job they can do, for example. Mrs Taylor worked three hours a day in the school meals service:

'Before I got married I was a nurse. I loved it . . . Sometimes I can get really nostalgic about it, like when I go to the hospital with him. I made up my mind I would always do it, which I would have done up to finding out about John. He was just getting old enough to be able to leave, because he was six when we found out [he had muscular dystrophy]'.

The need for flexible hours and sympathetic employers similarly restricted the job opportunities of this mother with an 8-year-old mentally handicapped daughter:

'[In term time] I just transfer on to the day shift and then when the school holidays come I go back to evenings. I've just been very fortunate in finding a job that will put up with school holidays and child illnesses and all the rest of it. With Samantha I'm tied to this job, I haven't got any choice. If I wanted to get another job, I can't, I'm stuck with this one. I'm grateful for it but you are limited. I'm in a better position than most, at least I've got a job. A lot of parents with handicapped children, well the mothers anyway, just can't go out to work.'

Effects on participation rates, hours and earnings

These are some individual women's perceptions of how their child's disability has affected their opportunities for paid work or caused alterations in their working lives. How general is this picture? Surveys of women with disabled children have invariably found a high proportion claiming that their employment patterns and earnings were affected (Woodburn, 1973; Burton, 1975; Baldwin, 1976a; Butler *et al.*, 1976). However, none supplied detailed comparative information on hours of work or earnings. A study was therefore undertaken which enabled the employment patterns, hours of paid work and earnings of parents of severely disabled children to be set alongside those of a matched group of families drawn from the 1978 FES. This study produced overwhelmingly clear evidence that severe disability in a child is associated with marked differences in women's participation rates, hours of work and earnings; and that these disparities increase as children grow older. This evidence is examined below.

Table 3.2 illustrates the differences in the participation rates of the women with disabled children and the women in the FES control group.

Table 3.2 *Employment status of the women in the comparative income and expenditure group*

Employment status	Families with a disabled child		FES control group	
	No.	% of all women	No.	% of all women
Working full-time	22	4.7	83	12.0
part-time*	135	28.5	253	36.2
Not in paid employment	316	66.8	361	51.8
Total number of women	473**	100	697	100

* Part-time was defined as 30 hours a week or less.
** 7 women were excluded because, although they were in paid work, the number of hours they worked was not recorded.

Women's labour-market participation can be measured in two ways: by whether they are currently in paid employment (as in Table 3.2 and subsequent tables) or according to whether they are considered to be 'economically active'. The latter definition also includes those who have held a job within a given time period. On this wider definition, the discrepancy between the two groups of women was even larger, with 35 per cent of the women with disabled children, as against 59 per cent of the women in the FES control, being classed as 'economically active'. The difference between the proportions of each group actually in jobs and defined as 'economically active' is itself interesting. The proportions of women with disabled children in the two categories is almost the same, whereas among the FES control a significantly higher proportion were 'economically active' than were currently in paid employment (59 per cent as against 48 per cent). Research on women's employment patterns suggests that, particularly when children are young, women tend to move in and out of paid employment as financial needs and family circumstances dictate (Moss, 1980). The data from this study suggest that the women with disabled children were much less likely than the control to have moved in and out of work in this way or to have had any spell of paid work in the preceding five years. This suggestion was supported by the women themselves, who frequently said that their child's disability left them much less free than other women to take short-term or casual jobs when money was short or bills pressing.

Whether women with children go out to work, and the number of hours they work, are affected by the number and ages of their children, and most markedly by the age of their youngest child. The younger the child, the less likely is her mother to work (Layard *et al.*, 1978; McNay and Pond, 1980; Moss, 1980). The prolonged dependency of children with severe disabilities suggests that while their mothers' participation rates and hours of work might not differ greatly when all the children in the family are young and dependent, they might increasingly diverge as children grow older. Table 3.3 shows this to be the case. When women were grouped according to the age of their youngest child, in each group fewer of the women with disabled children worked full-time or were in paid employment at all. The smallest differences were found between women whose youngest child was under 5. Differences between the groups increased with the age of the

Table 3.3 *Women's labour-market participation by age of youngest child*

| | Families with a disabled child | | FES control group | |
| | % economically active women* | | | |
	Full-time	Part-time	Full-time	Part-time
Youngest/only child:				
less than 5	1.1	17.8	5.4	26.0
5 or less than 11	4.7	30.0	13.2	56.8
11 or over	6.2	35.8	36.5	49.0
*Base figures	172		296	
	190		220	
	81		104	

youngest child, becoming very marked when the youngest child was over 11. At this stage 85.5 per cent of the women in the FES control were in paid employment, as compared with only 42 per cent of the women with a disabled child.

Among the women currently in paid employment, those with disabled children tended to work fewer hours than did those in the FES control group. The average number of hours worked weekly by the former was 19.2, compared with 22.3 for women employees in the FES control. A similar life-cycle pattern emerged, of smaller discrepancies when children were very young giving way to more marked differences as they grew up. The average weekly hours of the women employees with disabled children whose youngest child was under 5 was 16.4 as against 18.2 for the women in the FES control. Among those employees whose youngest child was over 11 this gap had increased to 7.3 hours.

The weekly earnings of women employees with disabled children were also consistently much lower than those of women employees in the FES control group—an overall average difference of £7. Table 3.4 shows that earnings were also strongly influenced by the age of the youngest child in the family, the greatest difference in weekly earnings being among women with older children. Table 3.4 also illustrates very clearly the different earnings profiles over the family life-cycle. The earnings of the women with disabled children

Table 3.4 *Average weekly earnings of women employees by age of youngest child*

	Famlies with a disabled child			FES control group		
	Mean £ per week	Standard deviation	No.	Mean £ per week	Standard deviation	No.
Youngest/only child:						
less than 5	17.3	13.1	38	24.3	23.6	93
5 or less than 11	24.0	17.1	68	26.4	19.2	154
11 or over	22.4	14.1	34	37.5	24.8	89
All families	21.8	15.5	140	28.8	22.6	336

increased much less as their children grew older, the difference between women employees with the youngest and oldest children being only £5.10, compared with £13.20 in the control group.

Differences in earnings were even more marked when the distributions of weekly earnings, rather than average earnings, were compared. As Table 3.5 shows there were particularly large differences in the upper quartiles of earnings among women whose youngest child was over 11.

Hourly earnings were also investigated to see whether differences in weekly earnings simply reflected the shorter

Table 3.5 *Quartiles of weekly earnings of women employees, by age of youngest child*

	Families with a disabled child			FES control group		
	Lower quartile £ p wk	Median £ p wk	Upper quartile £ p wk	Lower quartile £ p wk	Median £ p wk	Upper quartile £ p wk
Youngest/only child:						
less than 5	8.5	12.8	24.5	8.4	16.1	30.9
5 or less than 11	13.2	18.4	29.4	12.7	22.8	34.1
11 or over	12.5	18.5	28.9	21.3	30.2	48.8
All women employees	11.1	16.5	28.6	12.5	23.7	38.1

Table 3.6 *Quartiles of hourly earnings of women employees, by age of youngest child*

	Families with a disabled child			FES control group		
	Lower quartile £ p hr	Median £ p hr	Upper quartile £ p hr	Lower quartile £ p hr	Median £ p hr	Upper quartile £ p hr
Youngest/only child:						
less than 5	0.82	1.07	1.33	0.87	1.11	1.59
5 or less than 11	0.94	1.11	1.33	0.88	1.07	1.26
11 or over	0.88	1.05	1.17	0.93	1.14	1.98
All women employees	0.87	1.07	1.31	0.89	1.10	1.36

hours worked by the women with disabled children or also results from differences in rates of pay. Table 3.6 shows that in general the hourly rates of the women with disabled children were lower. These lower hourly rates of pay point to another set of consequences which follow from the restriction of the women with disabled children mainly to part-time work. A number of studies, notably that of Hurstfield, have outlined how part-time work, typically done by women with young children, is also associated with poorer working conditions and exclusion from pension schemes and other employment benefits such as sick pay and paid holidays (Hurstfield, 1978). However the majority of women with children have the chance of increasing their working hours or working full-time when their children are older and do in fact do so. Most women with a severely disabled child do *not* have this freedom of choice; they are effectively confined throughout their working lives to the highly unsatisfactory employment conditions of women with very young children. For example, 76 per cent of the women in the comparative study who had to take time off work because of the care needed by their disabled child lost money whenever this happened. Typically the bulk of women employees with disabled children accommodate their child's need for care by only taking part-time jobs. They thus become long-term marginal workers, permanently deprived of the privileges and protections available to the majority of employees.

In the following section we explore some of the effects of the restricted employment opportunities experienced by women with disabled children.

The importance of work

The opportunity to work outside the home has important social and personal consequences for women. Ungerson has suggested that while men view the home as a refuge from the pressures of paid employment, women see work outside the home as an opportunity to escape from the isolating and repetitive routines of housework and child care (Ungerson, 1981). It could be argued that if the 'daily grind' of house- work and child care is more demanding, onerous and restrictive than usual, then the significance of an 'escape' to employment outside the home will be of correspondingly greater import- ance. This certainly appears to be the case. Of the seventeen women who took part in the in-depth interview study for example, only four had no current desire to work outside the home. Of the remainder, six wanted to work but were currently unable to. While aware of the financial losses caused by this restriction, they also greatly missed the opportunities for a break in domestic routines and for regular social contacts, which previous periods of employment had given them:

'I used to get ever so tense and when you go to work it eases it off a little bit, you'd be surprised. You'd be surprised how it takes the tension off you if you can get outside. . . . I think it's more or less a change of company. You can sit and look at four walls for too long' (mother of 14-year-old spina bifida girl).

'As soon as Jeanette started school they said at the hair- dressers "Would you like to come and shampoo for us and help us out in the salon?" I said "Oh I'd love it because it would get me out". . . . I really did enjoy it, meeting other people and mixing with them. It was really smashing. . . . I just enjoyed getting out of the house' (mother of 8-year- old girl with spina bifida and hydrocephalus).

'. . . it was more for company. I found when I left that I

missed the company more than the money' (mother of
15-year-old spastic boy).

These feelings were echoed by the mothers who did have some
kind of paid employment at the time of the interview study.
While the financial gains were important, the overwhelming
value of their work outside the home was that it provided a
break in an otherwise monotonous domestic routine:

'It gives you that little break. I went back just for the
break, just to get out of it for three hours, and the money's
very nice as well' (mother of 7-year-old boy with cystic
fibrosis).

Paid employment was also a means of overcoming social
isolation because it provided a structured opportunity to
meet others:

'I think it's a break when you go out to work, because you
meet different people and I really look forward to going'
(mother of 8-year-old mentally handicapped son).

'But it's a break and you get out and you see the people
that you used to know. I get on well with them and I like
them' (mother of 8-year-old mentally handicapped girl).

The opportunity to meet people *without* disabled children
could be particularly important:

'It's marvellous because when I get to work I forget all
about, you know, Martha and James. . . . You're with
women who haven't got mentally handicapped children
and you sort of forget about it. You're in a more normal
environment' (mother of 4-year-old mentally handicapped
girl who also has epilepsy and cerebral palsy).

'It's segregation of parents; you ought to have integration
of parents, let alone integration of children. . . . This is
why work's such a blessing really—at last you're mixing
with people more of your own age' (mother of 6-year-old
mentally handicapped, hyperactive daughter).

None of the women interviewed in the small, in-depth
study was talking about jobs which contained many intrinsic

rewards or satisfactions, nor were any of them currently pursuing any kind of career. They worked in part-time clerical, service or domestic jobs; as barmaids, school meals assistants, cleaners, supermarket shelf-fillers and egg factory packers. Yet for those who were able to work outside the home there were clear social and psychological benefits; for those who wanted to work but were unable to, this restriction was a source of distress.

Although for some women money may be a secondary consideration, the ability to earn is also important. Having an income of one's own brings a degree of autonomy which may be absent when a woman is financially dependent on her husband. The lack of it can constrain a woman's ability to enhance her own self-image and self-esteem through clothes, hobbies or an independent social life. The ability to do and buy things for other people can also be restricted. All of these restrictions are likely to be disproportionately experienced by women caring for a severely disabled child.

The effects of not being able to work outside the home, or of reduced earnings, also extend beyond women themselves to include their families. A substantial body of evidence has now established that the earnings of married women are a crucial determinant of their families' economic welfare (Department of Employment, 1975; Doughty *et al.*, 1978; Hamill, 1978); an analysis of the 1974 FES for example estimated that the numbers of families living below the official poverty line would treble were it not for the earnings of married women (Hamill, 1978). Furthermore, the care of a severely disabled child often created *additional* expenditure: on food, shoes, clothing, bedding, transport, fuel, telephones, housing alterations and consumer durables. There may also be compensatory spending, to make up for any restrictions experienced by the disabled child or the rest of the family. The frequency and extent of the extra costs of disabled children have been documented in detail in the comparative study and elsewhere (Bradshaw, 1975; Baldwin, 1976a, 1976b, 1981).

Unless compensated by social security transfers or by a marked increase in men's earnings, the combined effect of reduced women's earnings and extra costs on families' living standards will be considerable. However, the comparative study found no evidence that men increased their earnings to offset their wives' earnings losses. On the contrary, there was evidence that severe disability in a child could also be associated with earnings loss among men; the weekly earnings of the men with disabled children were, on average, £8.20 less than those of the men in the control group.

Nor do social security benefits fully compensate for the financial impact of disability in a child. There is no benefit designed specifically to compensate for married women's loss of earnings or to pay them for the caring job they do. Children with disabilities themselves are eligible for two benefits: the attendance allowance, a general compensatory benefit paid to people aged 2 and over who need a lot of looking after; and the mobility allowance, paid from the age of 5 to help with the extra expenses arising from severe mobility problems. The total amount potentially available from these two benefits in 1978 was £21 per week; but only just over a quarter (26.5 per cent) of the 480 families with disabled children in the comparative study received this potential maximum. Just over a third of the families received less than £10 a week in disability benefits. Clearly then, social security benefits fall far short of the full costs of severe disability in a child and do not even approach the level of earnings forgone by women caring for a severely disabled child. Where such women are unable to earn, or earn very little, their own and their families' living standards must suffer. In some cases there will be real financial hardship; in many more, chronic financial pressure. And as children grow up, families with disabled children are excluded from the comparative prosperity brought by the presence of two full-time wage earners. After all social security benefits were taken into account, and with all the costs of disability still to be met there was a difference of £12.70 a week in the disposable incomes of the families in the comparative study whose children were all over 11.

'Yes, we are hard up because of Tracy. Because if you are parents with two children, at our age you should be enjoying yourself a bit after struggling for sixteen years. You should be reaping the benefits a bit now, but we

don't seem to be getting any further advanced than when
we started. To go out, it's an effort. Not because we can't
be bothered to go out, but financially. We haven't got the
money to go out. Plus the only person we have to look
after Tracy is my mum. And my mum is seventy now and
Tracy is just too heavy for her. No one else seems to realise
the tension you have. So we seem to row and bicker more.
Clothes we can't have, or a couple of pints up the road.
And we've had to pack up smoking. And make-up, hair-
do's, that sort of thing. I have everything when it's *really*
necessary for going out. I hear people say—my friends,
for instance—"Oh I couldn't *bear* to go into a chemist's
without coming out with some make-up or nail varnish",
and I wonder how they do it. I think if I hadn't to buy
these things for Tracy I could buy odd things for myself.
. . . And it's the whole family goes without. And holidays.
We've never ever had a proper holiday. We go off for a day
or two sometimes to a chalet his sister owns, at the end of
the season, but even then we take our bare housekeeping
money—no more' (mother of 13-year-old girl with cerebral
palsy).

Conclusions

The circumstances of women caring for a severely disabled
child of course overlap considerably with those of all women
with dependent children, particularly when their children are
under school age. They also overlap with those of women
caring for adult dependants. Consequently the policy implications of the issues discussed in this chapter are not straightforward, and involve complex conceptual and practical issues.
For example, while a *prima facie* case may be made for
providing, through a cash benefit, some compensation for the
earnings foregone by mothers of severely disabled children, it
could also correctly be pointed out that not all such women
would have wanted, or been able for other reasons, to take
paid work outside the home. On the other hand, the introduction of a cash benefit for the actual job of caring rather
than for real or hypothetical earnings losses is even more

problematic. While such a benefit would compensate for some
of the financial and opportunity costs of caring, it would not
meet the needs of women who want to work outside the
home and who are psychologically and socially deprived
because caring for dependants restricts their opportunities to
do so. Indeed, simply creating a cash benefit for carers could
intensify rather than decrease the isolation and monotony of
their 'daily grind' of housework and child care. It could also
reinforce the prevailing ideology that caring is a 'natural' role
for women, rather than opening out the possibilities for men
and women to share the work of caring and for both to choose
the mix of paid employment and caring for dependants
which best suits them. With these considerations in mind the
following broad policy developments seem desirable.

Firstly, whatever their marital status, women caring for
dependants do undoubtedly have strong claims to a cash
benefit both to replace lost or reduced earnings and in recognition of the value of the caring job they do. Arguments
prompted by the 1980 Green Paper on the taxation of
husband and wife (The Treasury, 1980) concerning the
future of the married man's tax allowance have, in a similar
vein, advocated compensation for earnings lost by all those
caring for dependants (Lister, 1981).

However, any development in this direction (such as the
extension of invalid care allowance to married women) would
clearly be inadequate and unsatisfactory on its own, because
a cash payment could simply justify and reinforce the isolation
and stress inherent in long-term confinement to women's
'natural' caring role. The following two developments must
therefore also be given serious consideration.

Firstly, there are strong arguments for increasing the flexibility of the labour market to take account of the domestic
responsibilities of both men and women. Job-sharing, flexitime and guaranteed time off, without loss of pay, for either
parent if children are ill or need medical treatment, would all
help to relieve some of the tensions which both women and
men can experience in combining breadwinning and parenting
activities. Legislation to bring about these changes is certainly
necessary, but so are changes in the attitudes of employers
and trades unionists.

Secondly, there is a need to develop attractive and flexible substitute care facilities for disabled children which accept and accommodate mothers' needs and desires for employment outside the home. Day care during school holidays and out of school hours is in very short supply—where it exists at all. Foster care schemes run by social services departments and voluntary organisations are slightly more common and in some areas are organised in such a way as to enable very flexible arrangements to develop between client and foster families. With adequate support and funding such schemes could develop on a much wider scale, thereby perhaps also bringing into public view some of the vast amount of work currently done without adequate acknowledgment or remuneration by the mothers of severely disabled children. Together, these developments would go a considerable way towards removing the handicaps currently experienced by women with disabled children and, indeed, by women caring for dependants generally.

CHAPTER 4

The caring wife

Judith Oliver

Introduction

This is not intended to be an objective review of the situations of married women caring for a disabled or sick husband. It is a picture of what they themselves perceive to be their situations. Evidence of their feelings about their lives and the way in which they respond to their circumstances has been obtained in two ways. Interviews were undertaken in 1980/81, made possible by a grant from the King's Fund Centre.[1] The interviews were non-structured and of various lengths from forty-five minutes to nearly five hours, in one case. The second source of information was the correspondence received before and after the establishment of the Association of Carers. Nearly all the letters and telephone calls were unsolicited and many of the letters ran into several pages. The majority of the wives said that they had never been able to talk about their feelings before and had given a great deal of thought, sometimes many years, to their situations.

'In sickness and health'

When we think about the restrictions which a wife has to face, we usually think of her child-care responsibilities. However, Anna Briggs, working on an Equal Opportunities Commission award, has estimated that at any one time there are more women caring for elderly and handicapped dependants than for 'normal' children (Briggs, 1981).

The government and various voluntary bodies have in the last two years become increasingly concerned about the stresses experienced in caring for an elderly person. The reports have come thick and fast—the Policy Studies Institute, Age Concern, British Association of Social Workers, all have produced work on the subject in the last year or so (Age Concern, 1982; BASW, 1982; Nissel and Bonnerjea, 1982). Within the current spending restraints, some improvements are being made in the provision of respite services. We have seen in some areas an increase in day care places, short-term or phased-care beds being used and the development of family support schemes such as the Crossroads Care Attendant Scheme. This interest and concern is very welcome, the only drawback being that 'caring' is now very often being identified as 'caring for an aged parent'.

The Association of Carers, established in 1981 to assist and advise all carers, believes that there is a widely ignored category of carer whose stresses are unique. They are deeply concerned by what is coming out of their contacts and correspondence with the wives of disabled and ill men.

While it can be argued that most carers did not have a choice about taking on their caring commitment, spouses can be seen as having least choice of all. When disability or ill-health strike there is a universal expectation—from the medical profession, social services staff and not least from the husband himself—that the wife will take on everything that is necessary. No consideration is usually given as to her own state of health, the other calls on her time and energy, her employment or, indeed, the state of her marriage.

A very frequent comment heard from wives in this situation is that 'I was never asked if I'd be able to manage.' This seems to encapsulate the attitude of professionals: the assumption that the ability to cope is bestowed with the wedding ring.

Marriage (and the marriage vows) purports to offer a unique relationship of mutual aid based upon an intricate network of dependencies, especially for the women. It seems to us significant that where the state *has* intervened to offer general support to the family (income maintenance or housing, for instance) the conventional roles thereby

> buttressed are those of husband and breadwinner. The
> state less readily shares, let alone takes over, the caring and
> nurturing work usually ascribed to the dependent wife
>   (Land and Parker, 1978).

Several members have said that there was no preparation time allowed on their husband's hospital discharge. Some were telephoned and told that they must come and collect their husbands; two were actually told when they arrived for a hospital visit that they could take their husbands home with them. They all feel very bitter that after, in most cases, months in hospital, the disabled person was discharged home without aids, equipment, community nurse visits arranged, GPs notified, time to arrange the home, prepare the children and so on. Usually no nursing or caring instructions had been provided.

One wife faced this discharge situation. Her husband had been seriously injured in a car crash. He was paralysed down one side, scarred and brain-damaged to the point where he didn't recognise his wife and children. He was epileptic and could barely speak. He was discharged from hospital at three hours' notice and it was over three weeks before any visit was made by any of the community support services. In the meantime, she had had to contend untutored with his epileptic fits, his inability to feed himself and, most seriously perhaps, three screaming children who needed a vast amount of support to accept their father in this new, alien state. All this, of course, was taking place in poverty stricken conditions, as the whole family was now dependent on minimal state benefits. It was a further seven months before this desperately damaged man received either mobility[2] or attendance allowances.[3]

At no time was his wife asked (a) if she wanted her husband (who was in no way except legally still her husband) to return to her; (b) if she would be able to care for him properly and (c) what equipment and services she would require to enable her to undertake the task. She felt, when eventually someone from the Association met her and was able to ask her about her feelings, that, panic-stricken as she was, she had vowed to care 'for better and for worse' and this is the dilemma most wives face and the situation which most statutory services rely upon.

Other caring relationships can better stand separation than can marriage, it would seem. The parent of a very handicapped child can see him go off to a residential school knowing that she is still his mother. Your parents remain your parents, even when they are living in an old people's home or hospital. But your husband seems to be a different matter. Most women spoken to felt that if they had their husbands 'put away', as they saw it, the damage to their relationships would be irreparable. In fact, they regarded this decision with the same seriousness as they did divorce, frequently equating the two situations.

This feeling of 'breaking up' the marriage extended to fears about the effects on the children of sending their father away. One woman said that she knew that her husband's illness, which meant that he really did need her physical presence for twenty-four hours a day, had had repercussions on her care of her children. They had been left to almost bring themselves up over the preceding three years and now in their early teens were being deprived of the opportunities which their school friends had, because of both poverty and restricted or non-existent mobility. However, she wondered how they would feel about her husband's going into a residential home, could one be found to accept him. Should she deprive them of a father's presence, even if effectively non-participatory, and should she allow them to think that one could just dispose of someone when he became 'inconvenient'?

Most wives quoted 'in sickness and in health' and, whilst admitting that they had probably felt when they took the vow that it was going to cover the odd bout of 'flu, could not see themselves breaking it when reality turned out to be far worse. Indeed, there is evidence that ill-health and disability are more likely to keep a failing marriage going than the reverse. Several wives mentioned that their marriages had been on the point of breaking up when the accident had occurred or illness been diagnosed, and that they had then felt that they could not in all conscience abandon a sick person.

'What state help?'

For the average wife, the reality of caring is that she is under pressure from every side. In addition to her own domestic role, she will probably have to take on all those tasks which her husband previously undertook or shared and then be a nurse or care attendant. All this, and probably the attempt to hold down a job, will combine to put her under financial, physical and emotional stress. She often feels herself to exist only in her caring role, as this is the only one in which she is acknowledged.

A major problem when working with wives who have become lacking in confidence is to try to help them to see that their needs are absolutely equal to those of their dependants. They have had to convince themselves in many cases that they are totally indispensable and irreplaceable in order, as one said, that they can see some purpose to their existence. If all the sacrifices have been made, social life lost, job gone, and she is then told that a volunteer or schoolchild, for example, is coming in to take over for half a day, then what in heaven's name were they all for?

A participant at a conference on caring very astutely said, 'When carers become completely convinced that no one else can do their work, they are awarding themselves the status which society denies them.' The state reinforces this perception of a wife's role by making her the 'pair of hands' which statutory services use as an excuse to fail to provide supporting services. Frequently, the presence of a wife in the home means that a man will be discharged earlier from hospital, receive fewer aids and adaptations in his home ('his wife can answer the door/cook his meals/assist him to the upstairs lavatory') and most domestic services, such as home helps, will either be forbidden as in some areas, or not offered in others.

Even the award of attendance allowance seems to be more problem-ridden when a disabled married man applies for the benefit. One woman, extremely distressed by the very intimate tasks she now had to do for her husband, like wiping his bottom, was told by the examining doctor that what she was doing was 'no more than any wife should'. She broke down completely when the doctor had left, and when her husband's application was turned down, forbade him to appeal, in order that she should not be put through such a humiliating ordeal again.

This leads on to a second benefit, invalid care allowance (see Groves and Finch, Chapter 8 in this volume), which is the only allowance available to the carer, as opposed to the disabled or elderly person. It is a 'two-tier' allowance in that it is payable only to a carer whose dependant receives the attendance allowance, but it would not affect the woman above, as it is not payable to a married or cohabiting woman (or certain others, such as women receiving widowed mother's allowance). This massive anomaly was compounded in 1981, when the benefit was extended to men and single women who are caring for a non-relative.

The reasoning behind the non-payment to married women lies back in 1948.[4] It was assumed that a married woman will not be economically active and will be supported by her husband. Even if this were true, and of course, the majority of married women do work, it is plainly ridiculous that the principle is carried to a woman who is not able to work because she is caring for a husband who is too ill to go out and support her. Many wives express their anger over this situation, frequently speaking of the amount they save the state and saying that to be paid nothing equates with being valued at nothing. They feel that extension of the benefit would not only be immensely useful financially but also some acknowledgment of the strenuous work which they do, and of their value to the state and exchequer.

It is in terms of assistance at home that most anger occurs. By seeing the wife as a person who will always be present, always free to assist and always willing to subjugate her own needs and wishes entirely to her husband, statutory services can avoid providing nearly all services. Adaptations to homes are felt to be greatly restricted in these circumstances. For example, if a kitchen is inaccessible to a disabled man, it is not seen to matter, as a wife always cooks for her husband anyway, doesn't she? If a bathroom is designed to make it impossible for a disabled man to go to the lavatory unaided, it doesn't matter that he and his wife have the embarrassment of her having to assist him as it would if it were a parent/adult child relationship does it? The work builds up, the stresses increase and the wife becomes a care attendant/nurse/cook/cleaner/weight lifter/hospital porter/chauffeuse/battler with authority and a 'difficult customer' to the statutory services.

These same services, when they do offer aids and adaptations, go a stage further in demolishing the marriage. They tend to have no thought for the differences in providing a home for a single person and one for a married couple. For example, if the disabled man needs a downstairs bedroom extension, it will usually be a single one—no space for a double bed. When a downstairs room, such as a small dining-room, is being considered for use as a bedroom, the wife cannot argue that there is not room for the marital bed. Expenditure can only be authorised in terms of the disabled person's needs, and if he has somewhere to lay his head, then duty is done. When a special mattress, such as a ripple mattress, is required it is only available in single sizes. It seems that the whole world is determined to regard the marriage in the widest sense as over. As one woman said, 'They've left me with all the responsibilities and none of the fun.'

'Have a cuddle instead'

Sexual problems are widely spoken of by wives. Some are caused by impotence following the disease or accident, some by extreme pain and some by impotence brought about by the side-effect of drugs. The development of organisations such as SPOD is not seen as being helpful to the non-disabled spouse. Several made comments like that of the woman who said:

> 'It may be all right to suggest alternatives to a full sex-life to someone who is disabled and knows that it's better than nothing, but if you know that there's nothing wrong with you and you could have a normal sex-life with someone else, it's just frustrating to be told you can have a cuddle instead.'

The loss of opportunity to have children is a bitter point with some. There would certainly seem to be some women whose lives are dominated by the knowledge that had they married another man they would be mothers. Adoption agencies usually will not accept applications, particularly where the prognosis is poor, and even when a child is very much desired, most wives made comments to the effect that if AID were available, they did not know how they would be able to cope with pregnancy and a brand-new baby in addition to the disabled husband. Certainly in those cases where a child has been born into a marriage where the husband is severely handicapped, life can be almost impossible. One such mother, who had been pregnant at the time her husband broke his neck, described the three of them sitting at the dining table, with her in the middle spoon-feeding husband and child.

More fundamentally, several of the interviewees expressed anxieties about the loss of their femaleness. They spoke of being 'de-sexed', of having no feelings of being a woman any more. Expressions such as 'neuter' were frequently used. It seems that several factors had combined to produce this effect. Firstly, as mentioned already, loss of sex-life; then loss of ability to relate to other women's lives. They saw their friends leading lives which were totally different from theirs —shopping trips, nights out, dancing, work, husbands who helped keep the home nice and who kept the family out of poverty, walking arm in arm and so on. It was not so much role change which they found difficult to cope with—most had not had very specifically defined roles before disability— but the fact that they had to take on both male and female roles. Many said that it would be pleasant to be able to ask their husbands to make a cup of tea occasionally or play with the children or mow the lawn, not from a spirit of 'poor little me', but in the sharing sense which they had previously associated with marriage. One woman cried because she thought she looked so physically repulsive now. She said she had huge muscles from lifting and pulling, damaged finger nails and a bad complexion from too much cheap, starchy food.

Another commented strongly on the problems of any outings. She said that it was often forgotten that the carer could only go to those places where her dependant could, and so poor environment handicapped both of them. She said that she had to plan visits well in advance, arrange transport and so on. She was particularly bitter when they went to her husband's former company's annual dinner and dance. She said that she hated all the other women who looked so elegant and cosseted while she was in a dress bought in a charity shop, a home hair-do and always arrived backwards and in a fluster, having to pull her husband's wheelchair up the steps to the hotel. She said, 'I know it sounds awful, but I think, "Take that smug look off your faces; it could be you next year." I find myself wishing that it would happen to them.'

A great sadness to all the women was the inability to join in family activities as their peers did. When the husband cannot travel far and most people's homes are inaccessible, one has to wait for other members of the family—grown-up children, brothers and sisters—to visit. One wife cried when she told of her elder daughter's pregnancy. 'She was so ill and I couldn't go to her and look after her. And when the baby was born, I wasn't any help. I didn't see the baby until she was well enough to travel and it was 3 months old by then.' To be a grandmother and not be able to fulfil the expectations one had is very hard to bear. What should be an enjoyable and relaxed time is one racked with guilt at not being around to help and sadness at the lost pleasures.

'The same sinking boat'

Despite the fact that there are probably 800,000 women carers in the country, the fact that it is difficult for them to leave their dependants makes them largely unaware of others in the same position. The EOC made this point in their booklet, *Behind Closed Doors* (EOC, 1981). The self-help groups formed by the Association of Carers seem to be helpful in enabling carers to meet others, to discuss their situations and to reduce the feelings of isolation. Women particularly seem to benefit from them and strong bonds develop. One wife described her group as, 'A crowd of us all in the same sinking boat. We act as each other's life-belts.'[5]

However, getting behind the doors is the first job and it seems that many professionals are still reluctant to put their

clients and patients in touch with each other for self-support.
Since many do not see the caring partner as being any direct
responsibility of theirs anyway it is *very* exceptional for them
to consider putting carers in contact. There are, we know,
some who do not encourage this to happen because they fear
they will be asked to provide alternative care when the wife
goes to the group, whilst others worry that heightened aware-
ness of their situations will lead caring spouses to desert in
their thousands, leaving the statutory services to provide
residential care. In fact, to date the Association has only
come across three carers who have actively tried to leave
their situations. In each of these cases we have assisted them
to do so, but in an orderly and considered way, making
arrangements for the alternative care of the husband. This has
meant that no crisis has occurred and the wife has felt able to
continue to be in touch with her husband. The usual situation
of a telephone call to the social worker or nurse, saying, 'I've
left him. He's your responsibility' has been avoided.

To feel detached from the world and other people is
immensely distressing and leads to mental illness in some cases,
drink and prescribed drugs in others. Even when the result is
not so severe, it certainly places an unbearable strain on two
people who are together night and day in an unbalanced
relationship.

Descriptions of the emotional strain in this situation are
legion.

'We sit and look at each other, with nothing to say because
we don't go anywhere or do anything to talk about.'

'The television goes on as soon as he gets up and stays on
all day. It's just moving wall-paper, but thank God for it.
We've nothing to talk about.'

'Communication is nil—I might as well be the cat.'

'Because he had a stroke, he can't speak at all and I sound
like a gibbering maniac when I get with anyone who can
hold a conversation. And then it's back home to talking
to myself again.'

A situation in which neither party contributes any new

experiences is claustrophobic in the extreme, and most of the women said that this was the point at which they began to feel like 'care attendants' rather than wives.

Several also made the point that they felt that their presence was counter-productive to rehabilitation:

'When I'm with him, he expects me to do everything for him—turn the TV on, make drinks, help him round the house. But when I have to go out, I come back to find he's managed all these things by himself. You'll probably say I should make him do more when I'm there, but I just can't face the constant rows.'

The necessity to have a valid reason to leave the disabled partner for a while is a recurrent problem. There are quite definitely some reasons which are acceptable—a visit to the doctor or dentist, a shopping trip for food and household essentials or work—and others which frequently entail bitter rows and are seen as luxuries. This sort of outing is broadly what might be considered 'social'—non-food shopping, the hairdresser, visits to friends, adult education. These are often seen as evidence of neglect and desertion and produce a great deal of ill-will. A wife who has managed to keep a part-time clerical job wrote to say how she lay awake at nights dreading her retirement, which was to take place in six months, knowing she would be expected to sit and 'entertain' her husband all day. Again, she also worried that he would cease to do anything for himself when she was there. Several carers said how guilty they were made to feel at wanting to go out, even when they could acknowledge that, within a 'non-disabled' marriage, these occasional outings would be the norm. Many have given up the fight, opting for the easy way out in terms of avoiding arguments. The self-denial involved cannot, however, be easily lived with.

A further aspect which makes it more difficult for a caring wife to continue to lead a life of her own, compared to a caring husband, is that it is still less usual, and particularly among the older age-groups, for a woman to drive. This means that she will be dependent upon public transport and its timing, and when her husband can only be left for a short time, this may be crucial. Outings together will also be far more complicated when outside transport arrangements have to be made. It is sad to see the family car being sold when the husband becomes disabled, when one knows what an improvement to the quality of life private transport can make. The time of most pressure on the wife, when she is trying to sort out finances, aids, services, probably house-removal, is hardly the time to suggest she learns to drive. This is a particular phenomenon of the coastal resorts. The newly-retired couple move to an out-of-the-way spot they enjoyed for holidays, and the fact that there are only two buses a week isn't relevant because they have their car, driven by the husband. Unfortunately, when he has his stroke or coronary a few years later, their retirement paradise becomes a prison for both.

'After thirty years . . .'

In terms of female caring, it seems likely that many elderly men are being cared for by their wives: far fewer elderly men than elderly women live alone (16 per cent compared to 40 per cent). 75 per cent of elderly men are married, compared to 30 per cent of elderly women. . . . Given the tendency for wives to be around the same age as their husbands or up to several years younger and given the traditional division of labour in the home, it seems likely that women are looking after their frail elderly husbands more commonly than vice versa (Finch and Groves, 1980).

The problems of the older wife are in some ways different from those of her younger counterparts. Whereas the younger may well have more calls on her time, in terms of dependent children or elderly parents, the older wife may well be caring in poor health herself. It is not uncommon to find, for example, a wife with rheumatoid arthritis caring for a husband who is paralysed after a stroke, or a wife with a heart condition looking after a husband with multiple sclerosis. The decision as to who is carer and who the cared-for is often difficult to justify in the eyes of the outsider, but usually one of two factors precipitates the choice. Firstly, the one who becomes disabled first assumes the sick role or, secondly, the one with the most dramatic or sudden onset of disability. So in the two cases quoted above, the wife developed her arthritis after her husband had a stroke in his forties, while the onset of multiple sclerosis, a dramatic, 'named' disease, was seen as more 'important' than a quietly failing heart.

These early decisions often make for the most ridiculous situations later. For example, a woman with Huntington's Chorea is looking after her husband who is a fairly fit and active paraplegic. Here, the late-life development of HC could not reverse the roles which had been established early in the relationship, though the wife is now patently mentally and physically less capable than her husband. One cannot expect, I suppose, that one day, after thirty years, the husband will leap out of bed and say 'Stay there! I'll look after you now!', but the implications for service delivery should be carefully examined in cases like this. This last couple were still down on the physically handicapped register of the social services department as 'Mr X—dormant case as cared for by wife, who will contact if help required.' The poor woman would not have had the energy or know-how to contact her doctor, let alone an amorphous structure like the local authority area office.

'If only there were . . .'

And what help does the carer require? The most common requests were the following:

1 *Twenty-four-hour access to community nursing services*
This has been laughed out of court by every Health Service personage to whom it has been put. The most common reason is, of course, financial, even though carers are saying that they aren't asking for trained SRNs, just perhaps nursing aides or attendants. One community nurse, however, said that it is not the role of the nursing sister to provide day-to-day care, but to 'assess medical needs and instruct the family as to how they should carry out the tasks required'. The common conception of every severely handicapped person having access to community nursing is quite wrong. Most

wives care for their husbands unaided or with, say, one visit
a fortnight to assist with bathing. When the disabled person
works and has to meet a time schedule, the community
nursing services are not usually available. (They seem to begin
between 8 a.m. and 9 a.m. and most employees have to be at
work by 9 a.m.)

Sometimes one gets a situation in which social services will
offer a day centre place to alleviate stress, and instead of being
able to use the place in conjunction with the nurse's coming
to wash and dress the disabled person, work scheduling
means that her visit cannot be arranged early enough to
enable her patient to catch the ambulance or minibus. So,
instead of receiving two services, one has to be dispensed with.

2 *Care Attendant Schemes*

There are now several of these schemes, the first in the
field being the Crossroads Care Attendant Schemes. These,
currently (May 1982) numbering forty-two throughout the
country, are usually established by joint funding and assisted
by private fund-raising. Each scheme has a co-ordinator and
usually about eight care attendants, non-medically qualified
people who replace the carer at times when she wants to go
out. The average help given is four hours a week and the
service is free to the family which receives it. The beauty of
the Scheme is that help is available twenty-four hours a day,
365 days a year and everyone who uses the service speaks
very highly of it. Not categorised, as so many services are,
into medical or domestic patterns, the attendants will do
everything from peeling potatoes to helping someone on to
the lavatory. All those tasks, in fact, which the family carer
would be doing at that time.

The other main scheme is the Cheshire Family Support
Service and there are several others working in small areas.

3 *Respite care/short term care*

It would seem that many short-term care schemes exist, but
that many are underused. This often appears to be because
they are not widely enough publicised. Most of the carers we
spoke to had not been aware that such schemes existed, in
Younger Disabled Units or Cheshire Homes usually, and

would certainly think about using them now that they know about them. The main drawback is that, while giving the wife a rest two or three times a year, they do not enable her, for example, to return to work.

4 Day-centre care

This is seen by all as having the potential to be an excellent service if the needs of the carers were fully taken into consideration. At present, where such centres exist, the 'day' care can be as few as three hours—11.00 to 2.00 for example. More commonly, they usually offer something like four or five hours, but this still is not sufficient time, especially as it is usually over the lunch-hour, for employment to be undertaken on the strength of this provision. It is unusual for care to be offered on five days a week, too, so this can also make total resumption of a normal working life impossible.

Where there is a good centre, however, life can be made much easier for the carer. Bathing can be done there, and hairdressing and chiropody services provided, shopping and education facilities offered and recreation and welfare rights advice made available. Additionally, conversation and new contacts make coming together again at the end of the day much more stimulating and pleasant.

5 Extension of Invalid Care Allowance

The extension of ICA to married women is seen as essential for two main reasons. Firstly, it gives married women some money of their own and secondly, it acknowledges what they are doing as being a job, and not an automatically assumed duty (see Groves and Finch, Chapter 8 in this volume).

'If only he would . . . '

Of course, all these services are dependent on their acceptability to the disabled person. Some are, for understandable reasons, quite unable to accept that their care is a burden to their wives. It must be difficult to live with the fact that one is entirely reliant upon someone else for all one's needs, and to know that this reliance is probably breaking that person's health.

An appropriate role for the professional is to encourage the husband to see that life could by much improved and revitalised if both partners can separate occasionally. It can also be pointed out that should a crisis arise—the wife needing an operation, for example—then alternative care would be forced upon the husband and that it is infinitely preferable for this to be provided by someone who is already known and who is familiar with his routine.

There is no doubt that some disabled people can become very adept at blackmail when they wish to influence the carer. Comments such as 'He always manages to pass out just as I'm putting my coat on' or 'He knows I can't bear to see him cry so I just give in and do what he wants' were not at all uncommon. The guilt which this engenders in the carer is quite devastating. Some said that they even feel guilty about their own good health. Women are particularly vulnerable to being made to feel guilty in any circumstances, and caring is an area where this vulnerability can be most played upon (see Graham, Chapter 1 in this volume).

In turn, it becomes easier to make-believe that the situation is one which she wants to be in, rather than one which she is fighting against, and self-delusion takes over. The Association finds that most carers are unwilling to speak openly about their stresses in front of the dependant and that many will not admit their true feelings even when unaccompanied. After a short time with other carers, however, they begin to open up and acknowledge their feelings and can then make a start towards thinking positively about solutions to their situations.

This again has implications for professionals, of course, If a quick 'How are things, Mrs X?' is all a carer gets, and that in front of her husband, the true picture will never be known. Since the majority of workers in health and social services see the disabled person as the patient or client anyway, then involvement with the carer will not usually be sought. The carer, knowing that she is not the direct recipient of services, is usually reluctant to seek help from those whom she sees as assisting her husband. Indeed, many carers have commented specifically about the attitude of general practitioners. 'When

I went to him for a tonic, he didn't listen. He just wanted to know how my husband was', is a typical quote.

Conclusion

Married women feel themselves to be taken for granted. They strongly suspect that their services are used as cheap labour and as a substitute for good housing, adaptations and rehabilitation. Eventually they cease to fight the system and their husbands, preferring to lead 'a quiet life', no matter what personal deprivation they suffer.

Whilst there is no evidence that marriages in which the husband is disabled break up more than when there is a non-disabled husband, the interviews with the wives here would indicate a great deal of hidden breakup of marriage, the partners remaining under one roof because they see no alternatives, rather than out of a genuine desire to be together.

However, the majority of wives do want to care for their husbands, do want to make a good job of it but *do* want some recognition and help.

CHAPTER 5

Single carers: employment, housework and caring

Fay Wright

Although the increased popularity of marriage is one of the significant features of recent times, unmarried daughters and sons still represent an important source of community care for infirm old people. It was estimated in 1971 that about 13 per cent of impaired old people lived with a single child, almost the same proportion as lived with a married child (Harris, 1971, p. 25). Caring roles are traditional for women, not for men; yet single men living with one or more elderly parents now outnumber single women living with one or more elderly parents. The 1971 census showed 413,000 households of the former type and 309,000 households of the latter type (Office of Population Censuses and Surveys, 1974, table 38, p. 316). The existence of this type of household does not necessarily mean that the parent is infirm and dependent and the census figures do not include households in which both the child and the parents are above retirement age.

The number of unmarried daughters available to fulfil a traditional caretaking role for their infirm elderly parents has dramatically declined with the increased popularity of marriage and the disappearance of a distorted sex-ratio in which females substantially outnumbered males in the first half of this century. In 1931 approximately one in six women in their fifties, the most likely age at which to be a carer, were single, but by 1978 the proportion had dropped to about one in fourteen (Office of Population Censuses and Surveys, 1980a, table 1.1(b), p. 5). On the basis of current marriage rates, the proportion of women in their fifties who are single can be expected to decline even further.

This chapter reports some of the findings on employment, housework and caring tasks of a small exploratory study of the experience of being a single carer.[1] A sample of twenty-two single sons and thirty-six single daughters was drawn from their parents' names being on district nursing records in one area health authority. The boundaries of the area health authority were such that it included three outer London boroughs. Interviewing took place between November 1977 and March 1978.[2]

Of the 58 parents sampled from district nursing records, 51 were mothers and 7 fathers. Women predominated partly because of a sex difference in mortality; they outnumber men by 4:1 in the 85 and over age-group, and partly because they are more likely than men to be very severely handicapped in old age (Central Statistical Office, 1979, p. 32, table 1:2, and Harris, 1971, p. 18, table 10). The youngest parent was 60 years old and the oldest 99. But only a few were below the age of 90. Three-quarters of the parents were aged 85 or over and a third were aged 90 or more.

All of the parents had multiple impairments. The most common cause of impairment, as in other studies of the elderly, was arthritis or rheumatism (Harris, 1971, p. 9, and Hunt, 1978, p. 71, tables 10.3 and 10.5.1). More than half the parents suffered from it. Deterioration of the sensory organs was common. About one in six parents were either deaf or very hard of hearing and about one in four were either blind or partially sighted. A few were both deaf and blind. Incontinence was a considerable problem. More than a third of the parents were described by their children as either occasionally or frequently incontinent. Almost half of them were described as forgetful or confused. There were several cases of extreme confusion with the parent failing to recognise either the carer or familiar surroundings. Mobility was very restricted and only three parents were able to walk out of the house unaided and go for a walk. Half of them were permanently housebound but a third could reach a car outside the house and go for a car ride.

The youngest carer was aged 30 and the oldest 75. There were few in their thirties or forties and most carers were themselves either approaching or above retirement age. Their mean age was 54. Three-quarters were aged 50 or more and a quarter were aged 60 or more.

It will be argued that for the single men and women in the study a relationship existed between the two spheres of work, employment outside the home and housework and caring tasks within it. The first section compares their employment situation and the second their involvement in housework and caring tasks. Finally, the contribution of sex role expectations to the sex differences in employment, housework and caring tasks will be discussed.

The following analysis is in terms of gender rather than class. As Table 5.1 shows, the class position of male and female carers, as measured by their own occupations, was different. This broadly reflects sex differences between manual and non-manual occupations in the general population.

Table 5.1 *Socio-economic group of the single carers, by present or previous occupation, compared with economically active women and men in the general population*

Socio-economic group	Single daughters	Women in pop.*	Single sons	Men in pop.*
Non-manual	80%	59%	41%	40%
Manual	20%	41%	59%	60%

*The figures for the general population relate to 1977 and are taken from the Central Statistical Office's Social Trends 1980, Table 5.9, p. 125.

Employment outside the home

The majority of the carers in the study, 82 per cent of the men and 72 per cent of the women, were below retirement age. Their employment situations were a stark contrast. Table 5.2 shows that all except one of the men had a full-time job. However, this was true for only about half of the women. Four women, 15 per cent of those below retirement age, had part-time jobs. Altogether ten women, 37 per cent of those below retirement age, and one man, were without jobs. Almost all of them gave their parents' need for care as the

Table 5.2 *Employment situation of the men and women below retire-ment age*

Employment situation	Women		Men	
	No.	%	No.	%
Working full-time	13	48	17	94
Working part-time	4	15	—	—
Not working	10	37	1	6
Total	27	100	18	100

reason. Three of the women, one in part-time work and two not working at all, said their own health problems had been a contributory factor. As the study is based on interviews at one point in what could be lengthy caring processes, it is likely to underestimate the full impact of parental dependency on women's employment. More of the working daughters could eventually give up work before reaching retirement age.

The employment experiences of the one in four carers above retirement age had been very similar to those who were younger. None of the four men had either given up work before reaching retirement age or had felt forced to retire by the parent's disabilities. But about half the women had given up work before reaching retirement age. Indeed one woman had scarcely worked outside the home at all. She had started work at the age of 14 and had been persuaded to give it up two years later because of her mother's poor health. At the time of the interview she was 75 years old and still looking after her mother who by then was 99.

On the whole, the women had given up secure white-collar jobs to care for the parent. They included a social worker, two executive officers in the civil service, an administrative officer in local government, a computer operator, a nurse, a clerk and two secretaries. As most of them were in their late forties and early fifties when they stopped work, the chance of being able to return to an equivalent job if the parent died before the daughter's retirement age was reached, was probably remote. With the exception of a couple of women who received early retirement pensions, those who had given up work received either supplementary benefit, or, if the parent was an attendance allowance recipient, an invalid care allowance (see Groves and Finch, Chapter 8 of this volume). The latter is less than the long term rate of supplementary benefit, so, unless they have a private income, recipients are also likely to have supplementary benefit. Giving up work, then, usually meant both a substantial drop in current income and in the size of the occupational pension which could be anticipated on reaching retirement age.

There were common elements in many of the women's accounts of the reasons why they had given up work. Often there was a precipitating crisis:

'Mother fell and could not get up because of her arthritis. She spent the whole day lying on the floor. When I got home from work I could not get her up even with the help of a neighbour. In the end I dialled 999 and some ambulance men came round to pick her up. Actually she was not hurt at all, but her nerve was broken. She begged me not to leave her at home alone.'

'I was working near home and I popped over for a cup of coffee. The ambulance was outside the door. My father had secretly arranged for my mother to be admitted to hospital. He wasn't prepared to keep on coping with her. That was it. I gave up my job then and there.'

Usually the strain of coping with a job and the parent's needs had been so great that stopping work was initially a relief. A common recollection was thinking that at the time stopping work was only temporary because the parent was unlikely to live long. But often the parent's condition seemed to improve:

'When I stopped work eleven years ago, I thought she would only last a year but she did improve and now she is 93.'

'Quite honestly if I had known how long it would go on for I would never have had her out of hospital and given everything up.'

Other responses to the parent's need for attention included working part-time, varying normal work hours and taking the days of annual leave as the parent needed extra attention.

The four women who worked part-time all suffered a loss of income. This could be quite substantial. A clerical assistant thought she was very fortunate in her job:

> 'I work a 27½ hour work instead of 37 hours. I work five days a week and it means that I never have to leave my mother alone for a whole day. I am really lucky because they let me use up my holidays as my mother gets bad turns. The pay is low but that's not the main thing.'

It was more common for women than for men to vary normal work hours. Three of the women but only one of the men working full-time did so. The most common work pattern was to leave home relatively late in the morning and compensate by working later in the evening because the parent needed lengthy personal attention or there was housework which could not be left until the evening. Mr Reve, a garage mechanic, described his daily routine:

> 'My employer lets me start a bit later because of the amount I have to do first thing. My mother wets the bed so I have to wash out sheets and her nightdress and put them in the spin dryer. She can't be left with the gas on any longer, so I make her a drink in a flask and put out food for her. Then I shut off the kitchen with a padlock on the door. I just work later in the evening.'

Working flexible hours might have to be paid for in other ways. Miss Alexander had paid quite a high price:

> 'I used to have a very good job in the city but I gave it up two years ago. I just could not work the hours they wanted. I took my present job because I can go in late after I have seen to mother. I know I have to work late in the evening but she needs the attention in the morning. My pay is much worse than in my previous job and there is no pension attached to it. Society is going to penalise me in the future because at present I am doing what society is telling me I should do. I will not have an extra pension in my own old age.'

Taking an official policy of 'flexitime' literally and consistently arriving late for work could be felt to earn disapproval. Miss

Baker, a civil servant in her late forties, commented:

'Because of all the things I have to do for mother I have
arrived in the office after 11 in the morning for years.
I work until after seven in the evening but I know that the
people I work with resent it. People are tolerant of those
sort of hours for a short time but not when it goes on for
year after year. I know I have never had any promotion
because of it.'

Several people who would have welcomed being able to start
work later in the day were never given the opportunity to do
so. According to these informants, their employers would
not, or could not, tolerate flexible working hours. This kind
of flexibility is more likely in white-collar than blue-collar
jobs. Because they were predominantly in white-collar jobs,
the women in the study were more likely than the men to
have the opportunity of flexible hours.

Housework and caring tasks

Housework can be interpreted to mean a wide variety of
domestic tasks. Three specific ones were discussed with the
carers: cooking the main meal, cleaning floors and other
surfaces and doing the main shopping. The women were
significantly more likely than the men to be responsible for
each of the three tasks. As Table 5.3 shows, almost all the
women, 89 per cent of them, cooked the main meal compared
with 41 per cent of the men. Only 18 per cent of the men did
the main cleaning of floors and other surfaces compared
with 61 per cent of the women. Most of the women, 81 per

Table 5.3 *Housework done by the carer*

| Housework task | Women | | Men | |
	No.	%	No.	%
Cooking the main meal	32	89	9	41
Cleaning	22	61	4	18
Doing the main shopping	29	81	10	45

cent of them, did the main shopping compared with 45 per cent of the men.

There were two crucial differences between the two types of household. Firstly, households with sons received far more support from the local authority home help service. Home helps assisted 55 per cent of the households with sons and 22 per cent of the households with daughters. The difference was not so great if households with a working son or daughter were compared: 53 per cent of the former were assisted by home helps compared with 35 per cent of the latter. This sex bias repeated that found in a national survey of the home help service.

> There are indications that men are more likely to receive home help simply because they are elderly and living alone: for example, 98.1 per cent of the men were able to go out compared with 67.8 per cent of the women: 29.1 per cent of men compared with 8 per cent of women, had no difficulty with any of the personal tasks involving mobility (Hunt, 1970, p. 424).

Working daughters in the current study were less likely than sons to apply for a home help. This was usually because it was believed that such an application would be turned down. Such a belief was not without foundation. Four daughters had been refused a home help at some point in their working career, an experience not shared by any of the sons. One of these women recalled:

> 'I felt I could not cope with it all any longer. I had my job to do all day and then non-stop housework when I got home. Somebody at work suggested a home help and I rang up. They said they could only let me have a home help for a month so I said there was no need to bother because that was not a lot of use. Somehow I managed to keep going until I retired. But I feel a bit bitter that there was no help at all.'

Of course home help organisers are not alone in assuming that female relatives can, and should, cope with the problems of dependency. For example, in a study of the career of a sample of people discharged from hospital, Blaxter commented that social workers and nursing staff assumed that if female relatives existed then no problem could arise:

> Some of the most obvious failures in ensuring necessary care arose because this assumption, that daughters, sisters and mothers will automatically provide it, was shared by the professionals whose job it was to recognise 'need'
>
> (Blaxter, 1976, p. 58).

The second difference between the two types of household was that mothers living with sons were far more active domestically than those living with daughters. This did not apply to shopping which according to the government survey of the handicapped and impaired is the task disabled housewives find most difficult (Harris, 1971, p. 78). Only one mother living with a daughter and one with a son managed to do any. But half the mothers living with sons did the main cleaning compared with only 6 per cent of those living with daughters and almost half of the mothers living with a son cooked a main meal compared with 6 per cent of those living with a daughter.

Some of the mothers had quite a physical struggle to do any housework. An example was Mrs Thomas who at 83 was severely crippled by arthritis and had badly ulcerated legs. She could hardly walk and was described by the district nurse as having become very senile in her behaviour, chatting non-stop about events in her life seventy-five years ago. Nevertheless she managed to vacuum, dust and cook. When met at the end of the interview, Mrs Thomas expressed concern because she could no longer look after her son well enough. She was upset because he now had to do some of her 'jobs' such as getting the vacuum cleaner out of the cupboard ready for use. Mrs Green only managed to cook an evening meal for her son. She was 93 and had been crippled by arthritis for many years. Two years earlier she had suffered a stroke which had left her with very limited movement in one side of her body. Walking was very slow and with the aid of a zimmer frame. Her son said that it took her an hour to get from the sitting room to the kitchen which was next to it. A substantial part of her day was spent in preparing and cooking an evening meal for the son.

There were also significant sex differences in certain of the personal care tasks which had to be done for the parent.

Table 5.4 *Personal care disabilities of parents analysed by sex of carer*

Parental disability	Parents living with daughters		Parents living with sons	
	No.	%	No.	%
Incontinence	16	44	9	41
Need help in bathing	33	91	18	81
Need help in going to bed/getting up	29	61	7	32
Need help in dressing/undressing	24	67	4	18
Need help in using commode/toilet	20	55	4	18

Table 5.4 shows that there was little difference between parents living with sons and those living with daughters in the incidence of incontinence or in needing help with bathing. However there was a significant difference in respect of three personal care disabilities. Parents living with daughters were approximately twice as likely as those living with sons to need help in going to bed or in getting up; approximately four times as likely to need help in dressing or undressing, and three times as likely to need help in using the toilet or commode.

Two hypotheses can be suggested for the fact that mothers living with sons were both more active domestically and had fewer personal care disabilities than those living with daughters. The first is that sex role expectations are one important factor in the extent of disablement. A daughter living with a father or mother would be expected to assume a traditional female caring role as the parental impairment became worse. However a mother living with a son would be likely to struggle against an impairment to herself to maintain a female caring role in relation to a male. Thus the point of dependency would be likely to be reached earlier for a mother living with a daughter.

The second hypothesis is that a mother with a really severe impairment would be more likely to be admitted to a geriatric hospital or residential home if living with a son than if living with a daughter. Because such high significance is attached to male employment, both the son and mother would be reluctant for a job to be given up if full time attention became necessary. Equally the parent would be more likely to be offered such a place if a son rather than a daughter were providing care. Townsend's study of the characteristics of the new residents in homes for old people does provide evidence in support of this point. Demonstrating the effect of family structure and composition on the likelihood of an old person's admission, he showed that a disproportionate number of new residents were unmarried, widowed or childless. When there were surviving children a disproportionate number had sons rather than daughters (Townsend, 1965, pp. 171–2). Unfortunately no distinction was made between married and single sons.

Sex role expectations

The sex differences in employment and in doing housework and caring were consistent with traditional sex roles. In an urban industrial society a high moral value is attached to the male work role; to quote Parsons, 'It is perhaps not too much to say that only in very exceptional cases can an adult man be genuinely self-respecting and enjoy a respected status in the eyes of others if he does not "earn a living" in an approved occupational role' (Parsons, 1974, p. 247). The strength of the moral value of employment for men is neatly illustrated in George and Wilding's study of motherless families. As part of the study, community attitudes were explored through a small survey. Respondents were asked their views on what a father should do to provide the best care for his children if his wife died or left. Generally a high value is placed on the care of children below school age at home. But because a father rather than a mother was involved, 78 per cent of the sample thought a lone father with children under school age should go to work and 96 per cent thought the same of a father of school-age children (George and Wilding, 1972, p. 38).

The single men in the current study shared society's evaluation of the significance of male employment. In response to questions about whether time had ever had to be taken off because of the parent, almost all of them stressed that the job had to have priority:

'I've never taken time off work because the job has to come first. If that folds up, everything folds up' (chartered accountant).

'The only time I have ever had off work was when the council workmen were here and I had to check on what they were doing. If my mother had a fall I do not know what would happen as I would have to go to work' (tool room supervisor).

'If she ever gets so that I need to give up my job, she will have to go into a home. I am never giving up my job and that's it' (clerk).

Sometimes a few hours had been taken off work because the parent had developed 'flu' or had had a 'bad turn'. Generally the sons were at pains to emphasise how slight the interruption had been:

'I've only ever had one morning off in my life and that's when I thought she had had a stroke. Well, the doctor came and said it wasn't a stroke, so I went back to work in the afternoon. The neighbour kept an eye on her' (clerk).

'I've only had the one or two half days off because of her when the neighbours have rung me at work to say she is poorly. But I've seen how she is and gone straight back to work. She has insisted I do' (civil servant).

Three of the men said that if the parent were ill a married sister living in the district would take time off her job to provide the necessary care. On the whole the parent's disabilities were not seen as threatening to the son's job. The one man who was an exception in the study and had given up his job to look after his mother had problems himself which had probably contributed to his decision. He had a serious physical disability and had also suffered serious mental health problems for several years.

That the single sons usually had less responsibility than the daughters for domestic and caring tasks needs to be seen in the general context of male behaviour in the domestic sphere.

All the evidence from previous research relates to married men. Oakley's conclusion from a study of housewives was that 'In only a small number of marriages is the husband notably domesticated, and even when this happens, a fundamental separation remains: home and children are the woman's primary responsibility' (Oakley, 1974, p. 164). This view is supported in Hunt's national survey of women's employment. Although 67.8 per cent of the working wives interviewed had some help from their husbands in the household, it was mainly in washing up and drying up. 'The general impression is given that the help received by the majority of working housewives is very limited in character' (Hunt, 1968, p. 130).

Although in Oakley's view, women may not actually enjoy housework as such, there can be no doubt that working within the home and providing care for other family members, whether adult or children, is an integral part of the female role (Oakley, 1974, p. 60). It remains an integral part for both single and married women. This responsibility within the home is so taken for granted that it seems pedantic to say that working women are also housewives; it is rather like saying women are women. This taken-for-granted quality of women's domestic responsibilities is illustrated by one of the questions used in Hunt's national survey of women's employment: 'Do you get any help with *your household duties* from your husband (other member of the household) or a paid help?' (Hunt, 1968, p. 129, italics added).

Although single women have been as socialised as married women into a strong sense of responsibility for providing care, there are strong pressures not to give up a job. Not least, a job provides both a current income and usually some kind of occupational pension. Often for many such women continuously looking after the parent would mean living at supplementary benefit level and sacrificing part or all of an occupational pension in the future. The fact that under half the women below retirement age were in full-time employment illustrates the strength of this feeling of responsibility to provide care. All but one of the women who were working expressed strong anxiety about whether the parent's need for care would allow them to continue. The exception, a lecturer in adult education, asserted her job had to come first:

'To me my job is important. My mother knows this and knows it comes first. If I could not do it I would be finished. I am not domesticated and could get no satisfaction from just running a house.'

For the other women the future of the job was always in question.

'You are always worried about the future. It's a question of how much more mother will deteriorate and will the authorities do anything to help if she does. You don't have a career when you have domestic responsibility. You are always worried about whether you will be able to continue working' (civil servant).

'There are times when I think I should give up my job or at least go part-time or work one day less a week' (personnel officer).

'What shall I do if my mother gets worse? Should my mother go into a home? Should I give up my job to look after her? But what sort of pension will I get if I give up work now?' (secretary).

Unlike the men in the study, several of the women reported considerable pressure to give a job up. Sometimes this pressure came directly from the parent:

'My mother just kept ringing me up at work and asking me to go home to be with her. I felt I had to give it up then. I had already given up a full-time job and taken one in the mornings to fit in with her' (former clerk).

'Falling like that made her lose her nerve although she was not really hurt. She begged and begged me to give up my job and stay at home. Actually she didn't think I was giving up anything when I stopped work. She thought I was lucky not to have to go out of the house and travel into the office' (former civil servant).

Sometimes the pressure came from other people:

'I went to talk over the problems I was having with mum with the welfare officer at work and she turned round and told me to give it up. But I didn't really see why I should' (civil servant).

'I've been late for work a couple of times because I have such a time with my mother getting her ready for the day centre. She can't dress herself and does silly things like putting two legs into one knicker hole or her cardigan back to front. The manager was dreadful to me about it and said I should give up work altogether to look after her' (cashier).

A sex difference was also apparent towards taking time off work to look after the parent. Most of the men had insisted that little, if any, time had been taken off, but most of the women seemed to have behaved quite differently.

'I regularly finish an hour earlier than everybody else so that my mother is not left alone in the house. My employer has been very good about it and I still get the same wage at the end of the week' (wages clerk).

'I regularly have to take time off in the winter for my father if he gets "flu" or bronchitis. But it isn't any problem, I am so much part of the firm' (secretary).

This sex difference in taking time off work is partly a difference between blue- and white-collar jobs, a higher proportion of the male respondents being in the former. But the type of job in itself is an insufficient explanation. The men in professional and clerical jobs were as adamant as those working in factories that time could not be taken off work.

Policy issues

Although many similarities were apparent between the daughters and sons in the study, there were major sex differences in employment, in the amount of work which had to be done in the home, in the amount of personal care tasks needing to be done for the parent, and in the amount of housework that the parent managed to do. Although some of the men had highly dependent parents, this was the situation for most of the women. It has been argued in this chapter that sex role expectations were likely to have contributed to the degree of parental dependency. However, this does not alter the fact that when the parent had become highly dependent, adequate support services were rarely forthcoming.

The 1981 White Paper on the elderly commented:

> Community care services play a vital role in enabling elderly people to remain in their own homes and in preventing or deferring the need for long-term care in a residential home or hospital. They also make a very important contribution to the support of families caring for elderly people (DHSS, 1981c, p. 43).

The home help service, day care centres, meals on wheels and short-term places in residential homes are local authority services which could potentially be very supportive to both working and non-working carers. As far as the home help service was concerned, more than half the recipients considered the amount of help to be inadequate and would have welcomed an increase. The likelihood of being assisted by a home help appeared to be related less to parental dependency than to the sex of the carer. Such a sex bias in service provision is scarcely justifiable.

Only three parents in the study attended a day care centre. But one in four carers both wanted some form of day care for the parent and thought that the parent would find it acceptable. However, day care, whether in local authority centres or geriatric hospitals, remains poorly developed. Yet day care is an important means of relieving the strain of caring.

Meals on wheels was a particularly useful service for parents when the carer went out to work. Nevertheless, it was not uncommon for a parent to reach the point of no longer being able to cope with the meal which had been delivered either because of senility or because arthritis or general unsteadiness made difficulties in carrying a meal to a table and sitting down to eat it. At this point the daughter was put under tremendous pressure to give up work. A different type of meals service with appropriate supervision is needed for parents unable to cope with the traditional meals service.

Regular short-term admission of the parent to a residential home or geriatric hospital can prevent a situation becoming totally intolerable for the carer. Although such places theoretically existed in the study area, access was very restricted. A substantial proportion of the carers appeared not to know about them and several, who did, reported difficulties in persuading the authorities to accept the parent.

Community care services need to be far more strongly developed before they really contribute to the support of highly dependent parents and relieve the strain experienced by both working and non-working carers.

CHAPTER 6

Care for elderly people: a conflict between women and the state

Alan Walker

Introduction

The purpose of this chapter is to examine the family care of elderly people. Of course when it is applied in this context the term 'family' is invariably a euphemism for women, for it is women who provide the bulk of care to those elderly relatives who need it. 'Community' care for the elderly, therefore, depends primarily on the ability and willingness of women to provide that care (Walker, 1981a). One measure of the importance of community-based care is the fact that nearly three times as many bedfast and severely disabled elderly people live in their own homes as in all institutions put together (Townsend, 1981, p. 96). Again the term 'care' is a euphemism for a wide range of practical support and 'tending' tasks (Parker, 1981). The provision of care or tending implies at least one relationship, often a dependency relationship, and I will look at both sides of that relationship. In order to begin to understand the nature of such caring relationships it is necessary to examine the meaning and growth of dependency and especially the role of social policy in its creation and maintenance.

Following from this analysis of dependency, secondly, it is argued that both women and elderly people (the majority of whom are themselves women) share a dependent status, which is determined in large measure by the patriarchal state. Rather than there being a conflict between women and elderly people over care there is a conflict between elderly people and their female relatives on the one side and the state on the other. Thirdly, I suggest that this conflict can only be resolved through a radical transformation in the sexual division of labour at work and within the family as well as in social policies. In order to facilitate this analysis it is necessary to look first at recent demographic and social changes, especially the projected growth of the very elderly population, an unprecedented trend which must inform any discussion of community care and social welfare (Wicks, 1982).

Demographic and social changes

The fact that recent official and public expressions of anxiety about dependency and the future of community care have been solely concerned with the elderly is in large measure a reflection of their numerical importance in the population requiring care and of the projected growth in their numbers. It is, at the same time, a function of the rising cost of residential care for the elderly. Over the last twenty years the numbers of people aged 65 and over have increased by one-third—some 2 million people (DHSS, 1981c, p. 1). The number is likely to continue to increase at the same rate until the end of the 1980s. The most remarkable projected increase, however, is among those most likely to require care. There are currently about 3 million people aged 75 and over and this total is likely to increase by 500,000 by 1990 (CSO, 1981, p. 64). A similar rise is projected in the numbers of people aged 85 and over. In 1901 those over 75 represented nearly 26 per cent of the total population over 65, by 1981 this proportion had risen to 39 per cent and by 2001 it will be 46 per cent (Wicks, 1982). About 17 per cent of people over 75 currently require some regular form of care, either in residential institutions or in the community. Six out of ten of those aged 75–84 and seven in ten of those aged 85 and over are women.

At the same time as the proportion of the elderly population requiring care is expanding other demographic and social changes, including the decline in the birth-rate, delay in the age of parenthood, increase in divorce and in single-parent families and most importantly, the growth in the labour-market activity of women, has reduced 'the pool of potential caregivers' (Moroney, 1980, p. 40). Economic activity rates among married women have nearly trebled over the last thirty years, until in 1979 some three-fifths were working (OPCS, 1980b, p. 5; see also Rimmer, Chapter 7 in this volume). Although the recent growth in female employment has been predominantly in part-time work the fact that working married women still perform two roles is bound to reduce their capacity to care for elderly relatives. Over the course of the 1970s the divorce rate increased four-fold and it has been estimated that one in four new marriages will end in divorce (Rimmer, 1981, pp. 31–4). One-third of marriages are second marriages for at least one of the partners and this division of kin network will have implications for the provision of care (see Rimmer, Chapter 7 in this volume). At the moment we can only speculate about the sources of care for the step-grandmothers and step-grandfathers of the next century (Parker, 1981, p. 21). More certain, however, is the fact that those elderly people who are currently divorced (2 per cent) receive fewer visits from relatives and are more isolated than other groups (Hunt, 1978, p. 91) while those who are single are more likely than others to enter institutions.

These demographic and social changes raise important questions about the future of community care for the elderly and social planning for community care which go beyond the concerns of this chapter (see Walker, 1982c). But it is essential not to get these developments out of proportion. In the first place, while the growth of the elderly population is frequently discussed, paradoxically in detrimental terms, it actually represents a major national achievement in putting an end to many of the causes of premature death (Titmuss, 1963, p. 56)—in childhood if not actually in later life. It is only the social response to increased longevity that should give rise to disappointment. Secondly, while there is a close association between advanced age and disability, the vast majority of elderly people are able to care for themselves entirely without help, or with only minimal support. The most recent source of data on elderly people living in the community (Hunt, 1978, p. 73) showed that the majority are not functionally impaired. For example, three-quarters said they could go out of doors on their own without difficulty, 12 per cent could manage to do so with difficulty, 7 per cent only with help and 6 per cent could not go out. Two-thirds could go upstairs without difficulty, 27 per cent with difficulty, 2 per cent with help and 4 per cent could not manage to go upstairs. Nearly three-quarters could bath themselves without difficulty, 11 per cent with difficulty, 7 per cent with help and 8 per cent could not manage to bath themselves. Capacity was related to advanced age—with for example, more than one-half of those over 85 being unable to bath themselves without help—but the central fact remains that the vast bulk of care in old age is self-care, provided by elderly people themselves. This fact directly contradicts the more common picture of a dependent and burdensome elderly population and it is to a consideration of this stereotype that I now turn.

Dependency

Public concern about dependency in old age is not new. It has been a recurring theme in post-war Britain and can be related directly to social and economic change such as in the demand for labour. With high unemployment, increased longevity, the decline in the birth rate between 1964 and 1976 and an established trend towards early retirement, it is appearing once again. Despite its wide currency, however, it is by no means clear what different authorities mean by the term 'dependency'. Five different conceptions have been distinguished (Walker, 1982b). Life-cycle dependency encompasses all of those not taking part in productive work. Secondly, there is physical, social and psychological incapacity, most commonly used in studies of elderly people in residential institutions (see Townsend, 1981, p. 113). Thirdly, dependency is used to refer to a curtailment or restriction of freedom on the part of an individual to determine his or her own course of action. Fourthly, dependency has been used to indicate reliance, wholly or partly, on the state for financial support. Finally, there is structural dependency, which is used to describe the structured denial or restriction of access to a wide range of social resources, including income. This taxonomy helps to distinguish the specific characteristics of dependency in old age. It is discussed primarily in relation to the life-cycle and especially in physical terms. Whereas, for example, dependency in childhood is usually treated simply as a feature of the life-cycle.

There are other differences in the approach to dependency at different ends of the age spectrum (Walker, 1982b) which underscore the different policy responses to the two. Dependency in childhood is a universal experience, with not only everyone having gone through it but also the majority of adults having experienced caring for dependent children (Moss, 1982). Most women expect to provide care for a young child at some stage in their lives. Dependency in old age is by no means a universal experience, although it has been estimated that between the ages of 35 and 64 roughly one half of all 'housewives' can expect at some time or another to give help to an elderly or infirm person (Hunt, 1970, p. 424). The fact that there is a large popular literature concerned with the care of young children and until recently hardly any to do with the care of elderly relatives is, amongst other things, one indication of this difference. Also physical dependency in childhood is 'a relatively short-term and diminishing condition' (Moss, 1982) whereas in old age it is likely to be the opposite. In addition to these intrinsic differences in dependency there are important social and ideological factors in the definition as a result of the differential allocation of value and stigma to childhood and old age (deriving chiefly from their relationship to production) dependency in the former is viewed positively and 'enjoyed'. Then there is the 'widespread belief that the proper form of care for young children is within the nuclear family, with the mother providing the major part of the care' (Moss, 1982, p. 7). A substantial literature, characterised by the work of Bowlby (1963) has attempted to provide a scientific rationality for this ideological position. Although they have no basis in fact (see for example, Schaffer, 1977), assumptions about the nuclear family being the proper place for the care of young children have exerted a considerable influence over public policy. One indication of the force of this ideology, as Moss

(1982) points out, is the relatively small and shrinking institutional population under 5. In addition there are, albeit
inadequate, income maintenance provisions for children, such
as child benefit. The care of elderly relatives has not been
similarly legitimised in social policy, for most of the post-war
period it has been predominantly a matter of tacit expectation.

One of the main unifying factors in these different forms
of dependency at opposite ends of the age spectrum is the
fact that the person depended on is invariably a woman. In
the case of elderly people with disabilities both sides of the
dependency relationship are dominated by women. But
women too are frequently 'dependent'. This description
usually applies to married women not working and is related
to the life-cycle of need, particularly child rearing (see for
example, Wynn, 1972) and its concomitant financial dependency. In other words, dependency often encompasses at least
two relationships. On the one hand, there is the dependency
relationship, between say elderly people and their married
daughters and on the other, the dependency relationship
between the daughter and her husband. Moreover, when the
structural bases of these different forms of dependency
are examined, a close coincidence of status and interest is
revealed between elderly dependents and the women they
depend on. The state occupies a central position in creating
and legitimising the dependency of both groups, often in the
form of social policies.

At the heart of the social construction of dependency
amongst both elderly people and women is their relationship
with the labour-market. Although the exclusion of the
elderly from the labour-market this century has coincided
with the rise in demand for female labour, both have been
used as a reserve labour force, to be called on when required
by capitalist enterprise and detached from the labour-market
when no longer needed (Breugel, 1979; Walker, 1982c).
Social science and medical evidence have also been marshalled
to legitimate changes in demand for these different forms of
labour and the exclusion of these 'dependent' groups. For
example, in the immediate post-war period, while the
concept of maternal deprivation was used to encourage some
women to withdraw from the labour-market, older workers

were being warned of the detrimental effects of retirement. The corollary to exclusion from the labour force is financial dependence. Elderly people are heavily dependent on the state for financial support, while women are more often dependent on men. Both predominate amongst the poorest groups in Britain. The social security system reinforces this economic or financial dependence through, for example, earnings rules and the assumption that the male partner in a couple is the breadwinner. In the words of the London Women's Liberation Campaign for Legal and Financial Independence (1978), 'This web of state regulations serves to hinder the development of women's social, psychological and economic independency by enforcing their dependence on men.' (Although the Social Security Act 1980 contained some improvements in the status of women, these are only a tentative first step, delayed until 1983, towards 'similar treatment' for women and men rather than equal treatment, DHSS, 1980a, p. 27.) Elderly women, especially married women, are in the most disadvantaged position. Elderly married women are less likely than men to receive a national insurance retirement pension in their own right and are much less likely to receive a pension from a former employer (Hunt, 1978, p. 28). Furthermore, the dependent status of married women under the social security system in earlier adult life is one contributory factor behind the certainty that, on reaching retirement age, they are likely to be poorer than men. Two-fifths of elderly women have incomes on or below the poverty line, compared with one-quarter of men and one-sixth of couples (Layard, Piachaud and Stewart, 1978, pp. 14–15). In other words, just as discrimination against women, and married women in particular during their working lives disadvantages them relative to men, so discrimination against women in the social security system superimposes on them reduced social status and dependency (see Groves and Finch, Chapter 8 in this volume). Closely related to these social security policies are those in the personal social services which have increased the physical dependency of elderly people and which have reinforced the dependent position of women. An example of the former is the regime in residential institutions (Townsend, 1962) and of the latter, the tendency in the distribution of services such as home helps to expect married women to care for their husbands (Land, 1978).

This brief account is sufficient to indicate some of the social factors which contribute to the creation of dependency in old age (for a fuller account see Walker, 1982b) and to show, moreover, that some aspects of the economic dependency of women can be traced to similar social forces. Both forms of dependency illustrate the close link that exists in industrial societies between 'dependency' and production. The social construction of dependency encompasses an extremely narrow conception of production, ignoring, for example, the important role that women and a significant proportion of elderly people play in supporting the more obviously productive labour of others (Land, 1976; Hunt, 1978, p. 101). Although not socially recognised in the form of wages, married women not in paid work are an essential feature of the productive capacity of a family and, in turn, society. Similarly with elderly people, families may themselves depend on elderly relatives to some extent (Butcher and Crosbie, 1978, p. 98). However, this 'dependency' does not imply inferior social status or stigma, which in capitalist societies such as Britain, is primarily associated with economic or financial dependence (Pinker, 1972, p. 168).

Caring for the disabled elderly

The majority of elderly people are not physically or mentally dependent. Most of those over the age of 65 living in private households do not suffer from any incapacity. But there is a significant minority who are moderately and severely incapacitated—21 per cent and 10 per cent respectively—comprising some 2.5 million people (Townsend, 1981, p. 95). To this total must be added a further 200,000 severely or moderately disabled people living in long-stay hospitals and residential homes (about 6 per cent of the elderly). For the majority of elderly people with disabilities the alternative to institutional care over the post-war period has been 'community care'. In the rhetorical language of politicians

both 'community' and 'family' are euphemisms for female
kin. Most elderly people living in the community either live
with their spouse (one-half) or alone (one-third), only one in
six live in other types of household (CSO, 1981). A third of
those over 65 have no children. Of those with children, one
in seven are living with a son or daughter. There is, of course,
wide variation in type of household according to age and
disability, with for example, two-fifths of women and one-
third of men over 85 (the age-group most likely to require
care) living without a spouse but with others, predominantly
children and other relatives. Those elderly people living with
their children or other relatives are more likely to be disabled
(Shanas *et al.*, 1968, p. 216). In 1968 half of all elderly people
who were severely handicapped and not in institutions lived
with a sibling, most of the rest lived with a spouse.

Family care and tending does not stop at those elderly
relatives living in the same household. The cross-national
survey of elderly people conducted in 1962 found that, in
Britain, 18 per cent of those that had difficulty doing heavy
housework received help from their spouse, 25 per cent from
a child in the household and 11 per cent from a child outside
of the household (Shanas *et al.*, 1968, p. 118). Only 9 per
cent received help from the social services. Family care was
even more crucial for the most severely disabled, the bedfast.
Thus some 16 per cent received help with housework,
shopping and cooking meals from a spouse, 65 per cent from
a child or other relative in the household and 4 per cent from
a child outside the household (Shanas *et al.*, 1968, p. 122).
More recent data from the official survey of elderly people
living in the community also shows that relatives living
outside of the elderly person's household are an important
source of care. For example, 19 per cent of those unable to
bath themselves without help and 21 per cent of those unable
to climb stairs unaided received help from this source (Hunt,
1978, pp. 75–8).

Women carry out the bulk of caring and tending tasks for
elderly relatives. A postal survey of carers by the EOC (1980,
p. 9) found that there were three times as many women
carers as men. The responsibility for caring usually falls on
the nearest female relative. Elderly people are much more

likely to be admitted to hospital or residential care if they are single or if their children are sons rather than daughters (Townsend, 1962, pp. 23, 27). In a survey of women's employment Hunt (1968, p. 109) found 5 per cent of women aged 16 to 64 were responsible for the care, to a varying extent, of at least one elderly or infirm person in their households, and 6 per cent were responsible for at least one person outside of the household (for over half of the women 'caring' meant doing virtually all of the household tasks). In her most recent report on the elderly living in the community Hunt (1978, p. 63) concluded that 'this survey therefore provides further evidence that the burden of caring for sick or elderly relatives most often falls on women and makes it impossible for them to work.'

The experience of care

I have already noted that most so-called caring consists of practical help and support or 'tending' (Parker, 1981) but what precisely does this entail? Until very recently there has been very little information in this country on which to base an answer to this question, but that problem is gradually being rectified by research (see preceding chapters in Part 2 of this volume). For example a detailed study of a very small sample of families caring for severely disabled elderly relatives found that the average time spent on care activities on week-days was 3 hours 24 minutes, of which 3 hours 11 minutes was spent by wives and 13 minutes by husbands (Nissel and Bonnerjea, 1982, p. 21). Fifteen of the twenty-two wives spent at least 2 hours a day caring for their elderly relative, but none of the husbands spent this amount of time in caring tasks. The inequality between husbands and wives was even greater in relation to those activities which are the most arduous and difficult and which put the greatest stress on those doing the caring. On average, wives spent 2 hours 30 minutes on these 'primary' care activities and husbands 8 minutes (Nissel and Bonnerjea, 1982, p. 21). Earlier research conducted in the USA (quoted in Moroney, 1980, p. 68) found that two-fifths of daughters living with parents who required care, devoted the equivalent of full-time working hours to that care.

Caring and tending tasks include physical work, particularly where incontinent relatives are involved, such as lifting, extra washing, cooking, cleaning and shopping, Then there is the mental effort involved in dealing with sometimes confused elderly people. Finally there is the burden of bearing the total responsibility for the provision of care and medication with little help from other relatives or statutory services (Deeping, 1979). Although many of these caring tasks are similar to ordinary housework it cannot be assumed that they overlap with other tasks. For example, the elderly person may not live with the relative or may require special treatment such as a diet. Moreover all caring and other household tasks may require greater time and effort because of the need to keep an eye on the elderly relative all the time (EOC, 1980, p. 15).

Providing care to elderly relatives often has a disruptive impact on family life and on other members of the family. One study of the family care of elderly relatives found that four in every five families were experiencing problems and two in every five severe problems. One-half of the families found that their social life was restricted (Sainsbury and Grad de Alarcon, 1971). This picture of tension between members of the nuclear family was confirmed by Nissel and Bonnerjea (1982) who found that in two-thirds of families there was considerable tension. As well as anxiety, physical and mental stress and inter-personal conflict the provision of care often results in a lack of privacy and strained relationships with any children because less time can be devoted to them. Moving an elderly relative into the family home in order to care for them can result in cramped accommodation for everyone, lack of privacy and increased tension between family members (EOC, 1980, pp. 32–3). In the American study referred to earlier families reported increased stress but also financial difficulties and having to make physical changes to their home. Furthermore, stress was related to the functional ability of the elderly relative, the more help given with self-care and household management tasks, the more likely the stress (Moroney, 1980, p. 68).

For the principal carers, women, often married women

with children, giving care can entail considerable costs. Not only are they subject to mental stress, but physical fatigue and strain as well. Some three-fifths of families caring for elderly relatives reported a decline in the physical well-being of the principal caregiver (Sainsbury and Grad de Alarcon, 1971). A majority of the women studied by Nissel and Bonnerjea (1982, p. 40) referred to emotional and physical strain, tiredness and worry. These costs are difficult to quantify but can have a deep and lasting impact on women and their families. The impossibility of taking paid work is the most frequently quoted direct and quantifiable cost of providing care to severely disabled elderly people (Townsend, 1963, p. 72; Nissel and Bonnerjea, 1982, p. 14). In addition to having to give up work because they could not combine work and caring (nine out of twenty-two women) all of those women in work (seven) mentioned difficulties that caring created for their work, such as being late and often worried about leaving the elderly person (Nissel and Bonnerjea, 1982, p. 39) (see also Wright, Chapter 5 of this volume). None of the husbands' work was disrupted. Some women have to change jobs or forgo promotion because of their caring role (EOC, 1980, p. 20).

It has been calculated that the cost of the time spent caring for elderly relatives comes to £2,500 per annum and that the opportunity cost of earnings forgone because of caring activities is £4,500 per annum (Nissel and Bonnerjea, 1982, p. 56). To this must be added the extra financial costs, such as extra heating, transport, food, bedding and so on usually associated with caring. It is not surprising, therefore, that carers often suffer from financial difficulty (EOC, 1980, p. 21). As we have seen, there are other less readily quantifiable costs, including leisure activities foregone, disruption of household arrangements and physical and emotional strain.

Caring for severely disabled elderly relatives then, often entails considerable direct and indirect costs for women. So far, however, this has been a one-sided account of what I had earlier established is a relationship between at least two people. Descriptions of caring from the perspective of the carer tend to concentrate, not surprisingly, on the sometimes considerable burdens of caring and present a picture of the elderly person 'taking over' the household (see for example, Nissel and Bonnerjea, 1982, p. 40). As yet we know too little about caring from the perspective of the elderly person being cared for. What is certain is that elderly people do not give up their independence easily, they are reluctant dependants. Determination often overcomes severe physical handicap (Townsend, 1963, p. 60)—indeed this resilience may itself be the cause of some strain. Elderly people desire more than anything the preservation of their independence, they desire 'intimacy at a distance' with their relatives (Rosenmayer and Kockeis, 1963). Two—or three—generation households require considerable adjustment on the part of elderly people as well as their relatives (Williams, 1979, p. 49). In addition, care is not necessarily a simple one-way transaction, elderly people are themselves the *source* of care for other elderly people. Thus in one study it was found that 30 per cent of the elderly were receiving help from others of their generation (Green, Creese and Kaufert, 1979). Next to a child living in the same household, spouses are the most important source of help for elderly people who require help with self-care and the most frequent source for those who are temporarily ill in bed (Shanas *et al.* 1968, pp. 114–15). Of course, in the vast majority of cases the spouse referred to was a female spouse (see Townsend, 1963, p. 70).

Elderly people also provide a great deal of practical help to their children. In Bethnal Green 59 per cent of elderly men and 87 per cent of elderly women were performing regular domestic or personal services such as shopping, cleaning, cooking and child-minding for others. Two-thirds of elderly women with grandchildren helped regularly by, for example, fetching them from school, cooking meals for them and baby-sitting (Townsend, 1963, pp. 62–3). More recent research, conducted in the Cumbria CDP area, also found that almost two-thirds of those elderly people with children were actively engaged in helping them by baby-sitting, shopping, lending money, and caring or cooking for school-age children (Butcher and Crosbie, 1978, p. 48). The extent of reciprocity is obviously related to disability and the variation in the amount of care provided by different age-groups gives some indication of this: in the national survey of the elderly at home 27 per cent of those aged 65-74, 14 per cent aged 75-84 and 7 per cent aged 85 or more said they were able to do things for their relatives when they visited (Hunt, 1978, p. 100). A further indicator of the importance of reciprocity in relations between elderly people and their families is the fact that the inability to reciprocate creates an unwillingness to accept help (Townsend, 1963, p. 70).

Having demonstrated that care can be a difficult experience for *both* women and elderly people, recognising that further research is required in order to reach firm conclusions, it is clear that both share a common interest in altering the current practice of 'community care'. The dependency of both is to some extent imposed on them by the absence of alternative forms of care. Elderly people are reluctant to enter residential accommodation, which not surprisingly, they associate with loss of independence (Tobin and Lieberman, 1976, p. 18). But while the whole responsibility for care continues to fall on one person, this prospect is likely to face increasing numbers of elderly people (a point I return to in the final section of this chapter). For their part, women have borne the often considerable physical and mental strain of caring alone far too long. In order to understand why this unsatisfactory pattern of care has survived without question until very recently, it is necessary to examine the role of the state in the care of the elderly. This suggests that there is a fundamental conflict between elderly people and women and the state, and between women and men, in the provision of care.

The social division of care

The family is the main context for the care of disabled elderly relatives, and within the family women are the chief care-givers. The reasons why women carry the primary burden of informal caring were discussed in Chapter 2. They also predominate among formal carers, with for example 80 per cent of staff in old people's homes and virtually all home helps being women (Parker, 1981, p. 25). The state occupies a central role in the maintenance of this pattern of care. Despite the existence of community care policies for the last thirty years, the direct involvement of the state in the caring functions of the family is still relatively small. Social services departments are primarily concerned with crisis intervention, short-term support and in cases of severe break-down, long-term residential care. The state is obviously committed to practice whereby the bulk of support for the dependent elderly is provided by relatives (DHSS, 1978, p. 6). In doing so the state tacitly supports the sexual division of caring. Without alternative forms of community-based care and while work and caring roles are sexually divided women are effectively coerced into caring, often because of guilt (see Graham, Chapter 1 of this volume). These feelings of duty and guilt can operate with regard to their husband's parents as well as their own. For example according to a married woman looking after her 81-year-old mother-in-law who had suffered from a stroke: 'Eventually she will have to go into a home, but I won't let them take her yet, as I would feel very guilty indeed. It wasn't a matter of deciding to look after her, it was really a matter of duty' (EOC, 1980, p. 13).

An explicit policy of 'community care' for elderly people with disabilities has been in operation for more than twenty-five years. In 1958 the Minister of Health stated that the 'underlying principle of our services for the old should be this: that the best place for old people is in their own homes, with help from the home services if need be' (quoted in Townsend, 1962, p. 196). This principle has been reaffirmed by successive ministers and official documents (see for example, Ministry of Health, 1963; DHSS, 1981a). In practice, however, this policy was compromised from the outset by the absence of strategic planning to achieve it, the failure to devote sufficient resources to achieve it and the reluctance of the state genuinely to share care with families (Walker, 1982a). Today the allocation of resources within the personal social services is dominated by residential care, which takes over half of the annual budget, compared with the one-fifth spent on community care. DHSS guidelines on community care services (which are themselves below independent estimates of the need for services) are nowhere near being achieved. For example the supply of home helps for those over 65 is only half of the guideline figure of twelve per 1,000 population. Provision has increased over the postwar period, but not in line with need: the jam has been spread thinner. For example, an expansion in the coverage of the home-help service has been carried out at the expense of the amount of service received by each elderly person. In the official survey carried out in 1976, 42 per cent of the elderly had home-help visits more than weekly compared with 64 per cent in 1962 (Bebbington, 1980).

In 1976, 12 per cent of those elderly people living in the community classified as being in moderate, considerable or severe need were not receiving a home-help service, 16 per cent did not receive a visit from a community nurse at least once a fortnight and 15 per cent did not receive meals on wheels at least once a week (Bebbington, 1981, pp. 66–7). Furthermore, the definition of 'need' in this instance includes only those living alone and who do not already get help with domestic care and, therefore, excluded all of those elderly people being cared for by relatives and others. The result of these shortfalls in services, the failure to increase resources in line with need and the assumption that if elderly people are being cared for they do not need statutory services, is that female relatives continue to be the main and usually sole source of care for disabled elderly people.

The state occupies a dual role in relation to community care: it may provide direct support where this is absolutely necessary, but its main concern is to ensure the continuance of the prime responsibility of the family for the support and care of its own members. So, as Moroney (1978, p. 213) has pointed out, by presenting traditional family responsibilities for dependants and the division of labour between the sexes and between generations as 'normal' or 'natural' 'the state supports and sustains these relationships without appearing intrusive, thus preserving the illusion that the family is a private domain'. Thus women and families continue to bear the social costs of dependency and the privatisation of family life protects 'normal' inequalities between family members (Land, 1978, p. 213) and constrains the demand on public social services. In contrast to the constant public debate about expenditure on the social services the privatised costs of caring to the family are rarely discussed publicly.

As well as giving implicit support to the sexual division of caring the state operates more openly to sustain it by the differential distribution of social services support (Finch and Groves, 1980). In social security too, the exclusion of domestic tasks from the attendance allowance and married women caring for their husbands from receiving the invalid care allowance reinforces the social division of care and ensures that many carers do not receive any payment for doing so (see Groves and Finch, Chapter 8 of this volume).

Two assumptions underlying social policy with regard to the family, as Land (1978, p. 268) has shown, are that men are not expected to look after themselves as much as women are and that men are not able to look after elderly infirm relatives. So, for example, elderly men are more likely to receive home-help support than elderly women (Hunt, 1970, p. 424). Also, while the population of old people's homes includes a disproportionately large number of unmarried persons and married persons without children, new residents with surviving children are more likely to have sons than daughters (Townsend, 1965, p. 171). The influence of social policy on the pattern of caring within families has until recently been underestimated. Not only do they confirm the 'correct' division of labour in care within the comparatively small number of families they intervene in directly, but also indirectly, within the majority of families. In other words, the principle of non-intervention in caring relationships has an important bearing on how families and women in particular perceive their role and duty towards elderly relatives. This aspect of what had been referred to as the 'naturally nego-tiated' relationship between the old and young in the family (Johnson, 1973), therefore, takes place within the context of the firm expectation that female relatives will be the principal carers.

The position of men in this analysis has remained secondary (reflecting their role in care), but of course, their interests are embodied in the state since it is they who dominate its institutions. The fact that there is a conflict between men and women in the care of elderly relatives has been demonstrated by the massive inequality between them: for every one minute spent by husbands on the most arduous care activities wives spend nineteen (Nissel and Bonnerjea, 1982, p. 21). But in addition there is the underlying conflict between men and women in the male dominated class and occupational structures. Although women's labour was socially recognised as an important aspect of the family structure in traditional societies (Lewenhak, 1980) in capitalist societies women have been assigned a low status in relation to production. This low status in the labour-market is a reflection of their economic dependence on men and the social construction of sex in relation to the labour-market. The elements of this social construction are familiar: the women's role is in the home and the male is the family bread-winner. This division underpins social policies in for example, social security (Lister and Wilson, 1979) and the personal social services (Land and Parker, 1978). The relatively recent influx of women into the labour-market has not altered the sexual division of labour. Women that do work are expected to perform not a dual but a *treble* role—paid work, caring for the nuclear family and caring for the extended family—and if they cannot sustain all three roles they are expected to give up paid work. Women in the labour-force perform these roles simultaneously and not sequentially. The experience of working women carers is of paid labour in employment and unpaid labour in the home (see Rimmer, Chapter 7 of this volume). Women's unpaid labour is privatised and not recognised socially (for example in the conventions of economic accounting) their paid labour has been predominantly in the low paid, low status socialised forms of family unpaid labour, in the social services, health services, offices and so on. There is, in short, a conflict of interest between men and women in the social division of labour according to sex in both the labour-market and home, and it is the resolution of this conflict on which the future of community care for elderly people rests.

The demand for and provision of formal care is socially divided on the basis of occupational class as well as sex. Townsend and Wedderburn (1965) found that of those elderly people in social classes one and two who were severely incapacitated, one-half already had a paid or local authority home help and nearly one half of the remainder said that they needed it. But only one-sixth of those in social class five who were severely incapacitated had a home help and only one-fifth of the remainder felt the need for it. The more recent official survey of elderly people living at home (Hunt, 1978) suggests that, despite a doubling of the coverage of the home-help service between the two surveys, it is still the case that those in the higher social classes are more likely to provide themselves with assistance when they are incapacitated (Bebbington, 1980). In other words it is the daughters of working-class elderly people who are bearing the brunt of informal care in the community.

Community care and the family: towards shared care?

The current social division of caring roles and responsibilities is not in the interest of either women or elderly people. The 'community care' of the elderly relies on women forfeiting other activities, including careers, and being subjected to considerable physical and emotional stress. Elderly people share the effects of this stress on women and the family and when the principal carer can bear the strain no longer the elderly person is likely to end up in a residential institution. About one-third of hospital admissions amongst elderly people were due to the fact that their relatives and friends could no longer cope, rather than because of a change in the condition of those admitted (Isaacs, 1971). While the state maintains a casualty-orientated care system it is effectively supporting this division of labour in caring and the effects it can have on both women and the elderly.

Both elderly people and their children want the disabled elderly person to continue to live in familiar surroundings (Dartington, 1980). So far the state has failed to recognise the need for an expansion in formal and quasi-formal community-based care in order to share care between the family and the state and within families. However, there are two opposing trends which suggest that the division of labour in care of elderly people between women and the state will increasingly be called into question (Walker, 1981a). On the one hand there is the growth in the numbers of very elderly people and the concomitant increase in dependency, much of which is manufactured by the state itself. On the other, there is the shrinkage in the pool of carers and in the time available for care caused by demographic and social changes such as the decline in the birth rate, increase in divorce and the expansion in employment amongst married women. But in addition recent government policies have increased the likelihood of a crisis in the care of the elderly. Chief among these policies are reductions in resources for the personal social services, when increasing expenditure is required simply to meet the demand created by the rising numbers of very elderly people (Webb and Wistow, 1982) and secondly, a worsening of family poverty and in low incomes generally, including those of elderly people (Coussins and Coote, 1981). In short, government policies have actually reduced the potential for independence on the part of both elderly people and women. It cannot be complacently assumed, therefore, that women will be willing and able to go on caring for disabled, elderly relatives. Yet the government have attempted to reassert the primary duty of 'the family' to care for elderly people and other dependants and to draw the dividing line between formal and informal care even more firmly. According to the Prime Minister:

> But it all really starts in the family, because not only is the family the most important means through which we show our care for others. It's the place where each generation learns its responsibility towards the rest of society . . .
> I think the statutory services can only play their part successfully if we don't expect them to do for us things that we could be doing for ourselves (Thatcher, 1981, pp. 3-5).

This ideology has been translated directly into policy towards the elderly: 'It is the role of public authorities to sustain and, where necessary, develop—but never to displace' informal and voluntary care and support. 'Care *in* the community must increasingly mean care *by* the community' (DHSS, 1981c, p. 3).

Policies framed on the assumptions that the role of the state should continue to be confined to crisis intervention and the family should be the main provider of care to the elderly suffer from two fundamental deficiencies. First of all, they reinforce the unequal division of caring between the sexes, and while one person shoulders the whole responsibility for caring, this role and the dependency relationship associated with it will continue to engender stress and fatigue. Secondly, they further reduce the independence of elderly people and their interdependencies within the family and wider community. Furthermore policies which, directly or indirectly, attempt to force the family to care for elderly relatives are likely to be disfunctional. Attempts in Victorian poor law relief to compel children to maintain their elderly relatives made them bitter about giving aid and reduced the potential for exchange among relatives (Anderson, 1977). (What is more, the aim of this community care policy is contradicted by the effects of other government policies which have *reduced* the ability of the family and community to provide care.) Also policies which continue to assume that care will be provided within a conventional nuclear family consisting of a couple with one or two children, where the wife does not do paid work, in view of the social and demographic changes outlined earlier, are likely to fail. Alternative policies are long overdue, policies which would ensure both greater equality in the division of responsibility for caring and greater independence on the part of elderly people. A full set of proposals on the former would go beyond the scope of this chapter, but it is essential that forward planning with regard to care for the increasing numbers of elderly people with disabilities should be related to the need to liberate women from the prime and sole responsibility for providing that care.

The economic dependency of both elderly people and women must be tackled through the labour-market, where it originates. Improvements in the status of older workers rest on full employment, job improvement, flexible retirement and the right to education and training. Similarly equality in family caring roles or parity in their negotiation is only likely to follow from equal access to the labour-market. A range of policies would be necessary in education, training, employment and child care. Both groups require the protection of forceful anti-discrimination legislation to protect their employment rights. When equal status in the labour-market is secured then income can be provided collectively for home responsibility as well as unemployment and retirement. The payment of such an allowance without concerted action in the labour-market would simply legitimate the inequalities in work and caring roles between the sexes.

Similarly with community care policies, if these are confined simply to supporting carers, even financially or in other practical ways, they will not necessarily question the imposition of the full caring responsibility on women, and may actually reinforce it. Therefore a range of policies are required in order to share care effectively. These would include action in the labour-market. In addition there is the recognition of the need created by disability in old age through a disablement benefit (Townsend, 1981) which would enable elderly people with disabilities to purchase care assistance. An improved attendance allowance which covers all care tasks, domestic as well as nursing, and is available to less severely disabled claimants would also give elderly people greater flexibility in their choice of carers. The invalid care allowance (see Groves and Finch, Chapter 8 in this volume) should be increased and enlarged to cover *all* carers and subsequently merged with a home care allowance available to anyone caring for a person in need of care. As well as sharing care with the family financially there is the need for services which support and substitute for family-based care. These services—including home carers, foster care, home wardens and sheltered housing—would be based in the community, would not presuppose that female kin will provide care nor that women will be more likely than men to be employed in them (indeed a positive policy would be needed to ensure that they were not), and would be orientated towards carers as well as elderly people. Some of the resources for this community-based care policy could be derived from a reallocation from residential care. Clearly this pattern of service requires not only a radical transformation of the government's attitude to community care but also in professional attitudes as well. Finally, bureaucratically organised formal care may not be sufficiently flexible to meet the needs of many families and it is important to encourage quasi-formal and informal care-givers. Again it is crucial that measures must be taken to ensure that this does not simply increase the burden on women.

The difficulties of sharing care between family members, friends, neighbours and the state should not be under-estimated (Parker, 1981, pp. 22–6). But there are some initiatives which suggest that it is possible to provide care to elderly people with disabilities in the community without increasing the burden on female kin. These include the Kent community care project, the Dinnington project and the Crossroads Care Attendant Schemes (Challis and Davies, 1980; Parker *et al.*, 1981; Bristow, 1981). But the need to share care more equitably between the state and family and especially between family members has yet to be faced squarely by policy-makers. Some other countries have come closer to this goal and provide some indication of the potential for shared care. For example in Sweden, families rely heavily on community services (Adams and Winston, 1980, p. 247) and Sweden has attempted with some success to co-ordinate labour-market policies with community care policies (Liljeström, 1978). If a crisis in the care of elderly people with disabilities is to be avoided in this country then care must be shared more equitably.

PART 3

The economics of caring

CHAPTER 7

The economics of work and caring

Lesley Rimmer

Should the costs of care be allowed to lie where they fall? This chapter examines one part of the rationale for the increasing emphasis on policies of 'community care' for various dependent groups—the frail elderly, physically and mentally handicapped children and mentally handicapped or mentally ill adults. In much of the discussion of such policies it is explicitly or implicitly assumed that they cost less than possible alternatives. In the first part of the chapter the truth of such assumptions is assessed. It is argued that such policies often appear low cost in public expenditure terms because they both fail to recognise *all* the costs of care, and, as a matter of policy, fail to compensate one of the main groups of carers—married women. The chapter then moves on to consider the private costs of care, both the direct costs in terms of additional expenses which families caring for frail elderly people or other dependants may face, and the opportunity costs. A large part of these latter costs is the loss of income from earnings when a carer is forced to give up employment, or to reduce hours of work or level of work. These costs have been underestimated in the past, and are likely to become more significant in the future.

Next an attempt is made to link these private and public costs of care so as to provide a more adequate assessment of the true costs of caring, and from this base attempt an assessment of the adequacy of resources currently devoted to community-care policies. Finally we look to the future. How far will the changes in the balance of the elderly population, the changing employment scene, and changes in family patterns affect the availability of informal carers, and the viability of community care policies? Above all, how do we ensure the best possible quality of life for both the 'cared-for' and the 'carers'?

Is community care low cost?

Even in the absence of the heightened political emphasis on the desirability of community care, much social care is, and has always been, undertaken informally and without formal recompense by family and friends (Rossiter and Wicks, 1982). But recently there has been increasing political emphasis on the desirability of policies of community care. What this means in practice, however, is not always clear. On the one hand the term community care can refer to a description of the services or resources used—for example, community care is those services provided outside of institutions. On the other hand community care can stand as an overall umbrella of policy objectives—for example community care for the mentally ill can represent all those policies which minimise the disruption to ordinary living (DHSS, 1981d, para. 2.2, p. 7). These two uses of the term are often combined in the justification of such policies: community care is seen as both preferable in terms of the quality of life it can provide in contrast to that in residential provision, but it is equally often justified on the grounds that the cost of community care services are less than those of equivalent institutional provision.

Examples of both these justifications abound. In terms of the quality of the care, Care in Action for example, asserts that 'there is little doubt about the benefits to be gained from providing for people's needs in a flexible way which maintains their links with ordinary life, family and friends, wherever possible and offers greater choice' (DHSS, 1981a, Appendix 2, p. 47). And the DHSS review of community care suggests that 'despite the hardship it entailed, treatment provided in the community was often more in accordance with the family's wishes than was hospital care' (DHSS, 1981d, p. 17). Similarly in terms of the respective cost of different types of care the sentiment that 'the whole community should be involved in providing adequate support and care for elderly people' is closely followed by the assertion that 'public authorities will not command the resources to deal with it alone' (DHSS, 1981a, p. 32). And in the same vein the National Insurance Advisory Committee noted that 'in some cases at least it may be less expensive for disabled people to be cared for in their own homes than in hospital or in local authority accommodation' (NIAC, 1980, p. 7).

While there may be good ground for questioning both these assumptions, especially for those who require near to continuous, intensive care, our purpose here is to examine the latter assumption. That is, whether policies of community care really are less costly and if so, why this might be.

At the outset it must be recognised that the information available to answer these questions is limited in a number of ways despite some notable advances recently (Wright, Cairns and Snell, 1981). For as the DHSS recently noted in its review of studies of relative cost 'none of the studies we reviewed assess *all* the resource costs involved in caring for an individual in the community, or even costs to other parts of the public sector' and 'in many cases they have not measured in their own terms all the costs which are likely to be involved or aspects of effectiveness' (DHSS, 1981d, para. 3.4 and 3.2, pp. 13, 12). This, however, is not an issue which is confined to studies of community care, but pervades many areas of social policy. And indeed a number of organisations and individuals have called for the development of a comprehensive system of monitoring the effects of public policy. Leaving aside these reservations, what evidence is there that policies emphasising care in and by the community are lower cost?

In their study, *Costing Care*, Wright, Cairns and Snell tried to account for the differences in the level of dependency between those in the community and those in various types of residential care. They found that the total cost of provision in hospital ranged from £105 per patient per week (at 1977 prices) for a new hospital, to £79 per patient per week. For local authority residential care the costs varied from £48 to £61 per patient per week, according to the level of dependency. For community care the cost again varied by degree of dependency and by whether or not people were living alone, and also by housing type. Their estimates of these costs varied from £39 per patient per week for a less dependent person in ordinary housing to £55 per patient per week for more highly dependent people in high-cost sheltered housing. For people not living alone, the costs were less, ranging from £35 to £48 per patient per week. Clearly these community-care costs are substantially below those of hospital care, and are on average below those of residential care. Indeed the study showed that in only 8 per cent of the total sample were community-care costs higher than those of residential care (Wright, Cairns and Snell, 1981, p. 34). Other studies have given similar results. As Wright *et al.* note:

> Despite (these) different approaches, and the different years in which the study was undertaken, all the work tends to converge at the same conclusion, namely that there are many fairly dependent people being maintained in the community at costs below those of either residential care or long-stay hospital care (Wright, Cairns and Snell, 1981, p. 39).

It is undoubtedly true than then *in public expenditure terms* community-care policies are often lower cost than the alternatives and also that this is an important reason for the renewed emphasis on them in the light of demographic changes. In the first place, 'it is easier to harness the energy and resources of the voluntary sector if people are in the community rather than in hospitals' (DHSS, 1981b, p. 3). And in the second, far greater reliance is placed on the contribution of informal carers, normally family or friends. Indeed 'the strength of the network of informal support available to people is often critical to the feasibility and cost effectiveness of community-based packages of care' (DHSS, 1981d, p. 54) and at the margins 'the presence or absence of informal care is likely to be a crucial factor in determining the need for residential care' (DHSS, 1981d, p. 30). In community-based packages of care then, the tasks performed by paid residential workers are performed unpaid by members of the family, or by friends.

Certainly it is not that the significance of this contribution is totally ignored, but rather that it is not 'priced'. Thus 'the "cost effectiveness" of these packages (of caring services) often depends on not putting a financial value on the contribution of informal carers, who may in fact shoulder considerable financial, social and emotional burdens' (DHSS, 1981a, Appendix 2, para. 2, p. 47). Although voluntary organisations, friends and neighbours play an important part, community care is in most instances family care, and within the family it is women who bear the main brunt of caring. In a study conducted for the EOC three out of four of those caring for others were women. The majority being daughters or wives of the dependent person (EOC, 1980). And this in fact goes some way to explaining why the contribution of informal carers is so undervalued. Many would argue that the battle to get housework recognised for what it is, often hard and unremitting work, has yet to be won. The same is even more true for caring. Women are expected to cope. Trained or not, fit and healthy themselves or not, they are expected to be able to provide sensitive and loving care to their dependants, and to do so without reward. There is, as another chapter explains more fully, a double burden for married women (cf. Oliver, in this volume). For while men and single (non-cohabiting) women who are forced to leave employment to care for elderly or handicapped dependants may claim Invalid Care Allowance (ICA), married women, along with certain categories of divorced and widowed women, are currently excluded from this benefit (EOC, 1981). By this exclusion alone the public costs of providing care are reduced by some £40 million (Hansard (Commons) Written Answers, 13 May 1982).

In summary then, there is some justification for asserting that community care policies are lower cost than the alternatives. But a major reason for this lower cost is that it is only the public expenditure costs of care that are being considered. The costs to carers are being ignored. Equally worrying, as the DHSS themselves noted, 'the community alternative might only appear cheap because its level of provision could be considered inadequate' (DHSS, 1981d, para. 3.27, p. 20). The inadequacy of support services for carers may well increase the physical and emotional costs of caring which are

documented elsewhere in this volume. In addition to the
social and emotional costs, on which it is often difficult to put
a value, there are a number of other direct and opportunity
costs to the carer which are now considered.

The costs to the carer

What are the costs of caring to the carer? Studies of carers
and their families have shown that these costs are of two
types, first the direct cost of extra expenses which handicapped or frail dependants may entail. For the frail elderly
there may be additional costs in terms of special diets, or
extra heating; for the confused elderly there may be extra
costs associated with 'granny sitting'; and there are of course
extra costs associated with incontinence, and the extra wear
and tear on clothing and furniture associated with some
physical handicaps (Baldwin, 1976a; Hyman, 1977). In
addition to these costs there are also the costs to carers in
terms of foregone earnings, when they give up work or reduce
their hours of work to accommodate their caring responsibilities, and it is these which are the focus of this part of the
chapter. In considering the argument that entitlement to
Invalid Care Allowance be extended to married women the
National Insurance Advisory Committee was advised by
DHSS that 'married and cohabiting women ... have the
support of their partner's income' (NIAC, 1980, p. 5). This
not only denies title to benefit to one of the major groups
providing care, but also reaffirms the assumptions about
women's employment which are so prevalent in the social
security and taxation systems. In both these systems the
earnings of a working wife are assumed to be subsidiary to
those of her husband. While in many cases this must be true
(women's earnings having fallen back from around 76 per
cent of men's earnings on average in the mid-1970s to some
74 per cent) the significance of women's earnings to family
incomes should not be underestimated (Hamill, 1978). We
know for example that households in which women work
are, if their earnings are excluded, poorer on average than
other households, and were it not for the wife's earnings

some three or four times more families would be in poverty
(Hamill, 1978; McNay and Pond, 1980) and while breadwinner wives remain a fairly small minority their numbers
are increasing. Between 1968 and 1977, for example, the
proportion of women who earned as much or more than their
husbands increased from 3.6 per cent to 8 per cent and if the
analysis were confined to women working full time whose
husbands were employed, this rose from 5 per cent to 14.5
per cent (Elias, 1980b). And the 1980 Family Expenditure
Survey shows that in non-retired households where there are
no dependent children and the wife works, her earnings made
up nearly a third of the household's income from wages and
salaries. In these households average weekly earnings of the
wife were over half that of the husband. For similar households with dependent children the contribution is less but
still substantial: one-fifth of the household's income from
wages and salaries and a wage a quarter of the husband
(Department of Employment, 1982, pp. 108, 109). More
generally, a now dated study shows that the earnings of
a third of wives make up some 30–50 per cent of family
incomes (Hamill, 1978).

But in order to assess the opportunity costs of giving up
work to care, we need to show both that the caring does have
an impact on women's employment behaviour and then
attempt to estimate the loss of earnings that this entails.

Employment consequences

In the absence of a national survey of carers the evidence
on the impact of caring on employment behaviour needs to
be pieced together from a number of sources. Hunt's now
dated survey of women's employment found that women
responsible for the care of elderly and infirm persons were
less likely to be working than others, and if they were working
they were more likely to be working part-time (Hunt, 1970,
p. 112). Similarly Cartwright's study of those caring for the
dying found that one-quarter of the principal carers gave up
work altogether to do so. In the case of working wives,
47 per cent gave up entirely and 36 per cent had to shorten

their hours of work. For daughters living with a dying parent 23 per cent gave up entirely and 67 per cent altered or shortened their hours (Cartwright, Hockey and Anderson, 1973, quoted in EOC, 1982b, p. 21).

Again Baldwin's study of families caring for a handicapped child at home found that the mothers were less likely to be working than mothers in other families (Baldwin, 1976a). And Hyman's study of the costs of disablement showed that over a quarter of those caring for the severely disabled had had to give up work (Hyman, 1977, p. 81). Similarly a national study of the long-term sick found that most wives of the long-term sick were not working (Martin and Morgan, 1975, p. 34). And one econometric study found that the presence of elderly members in the household reduced the likelihood of married women's labour-force participation by some 6 per cent for each elderly person (Greenhalgh, 1980, p. 308).

In some instances giving up work to care will in effect be early retirement. Hunt's survey of elderly people, for example, showed that among women who gave up work between the ages of 40 and 59 the need to do so to look after others (not including their husbands) came second only to their own poor health as a reason for giving up (Hunt, 1978, p. 63). And Parker's study of retirement showed that while only 3 per cent of women mentioned their husband's retirement as a main reason for their own, a similar proportion gave family commitments, and twice as many mentioned the health of family members (S. Parker, 1980, p. 12). Significantly, Parker found that of those who had worked since the age of 45, 24 per cent of the women but only 3 per cent of the men under pensionable age gave 'family/household commitments' as the reason they were not seeking work at the time of interview (S. Parker, 1980, table A5.19, p. 76). Such early retirement may increase the risk of poverty in old age, and particularly at present the probability of re-employment for the older age groups is very low (Walker, 1981b, p. 23). But if caring responsibilities occur earlier in the working life time, then giving up work to care may interrupt career progression or may force people to reject promotion, especially when, as it often does, promotion entails geographical mobility.

Even if carers do not actually give up paid employment they may need to alter or reduce hours of work (cf. Wright, Chapter 5 in this volume). Some evidence of this has already been noted (Hunt, 1970, and Cartwright *et al.*, 1973, for example), and Greenhalgh's study suggested that the presence in the household of a dependant with poor health could reduce the annual hours of work by more than 11 per cent (Greenhalgh, 1980, p. 308). More tentatively it can also be expected that caring responsibilities will affect the *type* of work carers can undertake. This has already been convincingly demonstrated in the case of responsibility for children by studies of factory workers (Shimmin *et al.*, 1981) and home workers (Hakim, 1980).

It seems likely that this finding will also hold for other types of carer. In particular, the need to limit the number of hours away from the home or to return home at lunch time may limit the amount of travelling time that can be undertaken. Again, carers may need to reject jobs which would require frequent travel away from home or involve irregular or unpredictable hours. Leaving work, reducing hours, or restricting the range of employment opportunities can have both short- and long-term consequences for carers. In the first instance, and most obviously, it can lead to loss of current income, and a number of studies have tried to estimate this loss. Hyman, for example, calculated that the average loss to carers who have to give up work altogether was £120 per week, or £6,000 per annum at 1980 prices (Hyman, 1977, quoted in EOC, 1982a), while Nissel in her small scale study estimated the lost earnings of those who gave up work as £4,500 per annum (Nissel and Bonnerjea, 1982, p. 56). Even those who remain in employment can suffer income loss through reductions or changes in hours. Baldwin's study of families with handicapped children estimated this loss to be of the order of £42 per week at 1980 prices, or some £2,000 per annum (Baldwin, quoted in EOC, 1982a, p. 22). This is closely comparable to Nissel's estimate of £1,900 for carers in her sample.

Those who are forced to undertake part-time work also suffer costs common to part-timers. While there is still some debate about whether or not part-timers and full-timers in comparable work are paid at different rates, there is no doubt that part-time job opportunities are at present limited to lower grade work, with fewer opportunities for advancement. Nissel, for example, claimed that part-time women workers were having to take up menial jobs in the secondary labour market at hours and in places designed to fit in with their home commitments. This can have costs not only in levels of pay, but in terms of the availability of what are misleadingly called fringe benefits. A major study of firms employing women showed, for example, that part-time workers were less likely to be eligible for employer's sick pay or to be members of the Occupational Pension Scheme (McIntosh, 1980).

Obviously the opportunity costs are not uniform for all carers. The loss to the individual will depend to some extent on their stage in the life-cycle (earnings normally rise to a peak at some point in the life-cycle, and then flatten off), and on other determinants of their potential earnings (their educational level or occupation, for example) (RCDIW, 1979). Hence financial incentives to return to work or to full-time work will differ from individual to individual. Nissel found that the earnings of those who would like to return to work were much higher than the average, and those who were not interested in returning were much lower than the average for the group as a whole (Nissel and Bonnerjea, 1982, p. 55).

Longer term costs

These then are the short-term economic consequences of caring in relation to employment. But what of the longer term? It is worth emphasising that caring may not be a short-term responsibility. In the EOC's 1978 survey nearly half the sample had been caring for five years or more and almost a quarter for over ten years. Only one in eight carers had been such for less than one year at the time of the survey, and a further one in eight had been caring for more than fifteen years (EOC, 1980, p. 11).

It is clear then that estimates of the *total* income loss to carers need to take account of the length of time during

which earnings are forgone or limited by caring responsibilities. But such long periods away from the labour market
will in themselves have an impact—parallel to that of women
who have been staying at home to care for children—somewhat
ungraciously known as 'married women returners'. Women out
of the labour-market for substantial periods may experience
particular problems in re-entering it, because their skills are
rusty or even obsolete, and whereas firms or government
training schemes may well consider women returning after
caring for children as an economic proposition, in terms of
investing training resources in them, this is less likely to
be so in the case of older women. This is a particularly acute
problem in times of rapid technological change. Perhaps this
is part of the explanation why on-going research is seeming to
suggest that interrupted employment profiles, of themselves,
have longer term consequences in the form of lower earnings,
or less senior employment (Greenhalgh and Stewart, 1981,
quoted in Joshi and Owen, 1981, p. 82).

Occupational benefits

In the longer term, too, caring may have important implications for entitlement to occupational benefits. An increasing
proportion of workers will become entitled to an earnings
related pension, either under the state scheme, or through
occupational pension schemes. There is already widespread
concern about the impact of leaving a particular employer on
the loss of occupational pension rights, and this is likely to
affect women disproportionately (Occupational Pensions
Board, 1981). Equally the Home Responsibilities Protection
of basic pension rights, offered under the 1975 legislation,
still has a number of inadequacies. Home Responsibilities
Protection is one of the benefits of receipt of Invalid Care
Allowance (ICA), but at the present time (May 1982), since
receipt of ICA is linked to receipt of Attendance Allowance
by the dependant, ICA stops as does Attendance Allowance
when a dependant has been in hospital for four weeks or
more. If this happens, the carer loses Home Responsibilities
Protection for the whole of that year (EOC, 1982b, p. 14).

The caring cycle

So far this chapter has been concerned with the impact of caring as though it were an isolated—if in many cases extended —incident. But it is becoming increasingly clear that women can be caught in a *caring cycle*: caring for children, for elderly relatives and then for aged spouses. Caring for children comes relatively early in a woman's life: the majority of mothers are in their 20s and will have completed the most intensive period of child rearing by the time they are 35. But just as the children are growing up and their effect on their mother's employment is reduced, women are increasingly likely to find themselves caring for elderly relatives. In the EOC survey, 90 per cent of daughters caring for elderly parents were aged less than 54, and half of these carers were in the age group 45-54. But then later in life women may need to care for their husbands as they themselves are becoming frail. Over 60 per cent of the caring wives in the EOC survey were over 55 and nearly half were in the age group 54-64 (EOC, 1980, table 7, p. 1). It is not unlikely that women will experience all three periods of caring responsibility. Ninety per cent of married women will, if present trends continue, have children and increasing numbers of women will become responsible for elderly parents.

Hunt's 1965 survey of women's employment showed that one working woman in ten and one non-working woman in eight was responsible for the care of at least one elderly or infirm person (Hunt, 1968, p. 109). Two years later, on the basis of a national survey of home helps, Hunt suggested that between the ages of 35 and 64 one in two housewives (that is, the person other than a domestic servant who is responsible for most of the domestic duties) could expect at some time or other to give some help to elderly or infirm persons. Her study also showed that one in five housewives aged between 35 and 49 years had a disabled person or someone aged 65 in the household. Among those aged between 50 and 64 this was true of one in four (Hunt, 1970, p. 424). Since that time the number of very elderly people has increased considerably and very recently, a small scale study in the north-east identified more 'carers' of handicapped or elderly dependants than there were mothers of children under 16 (Briggs, 1981).

The likelihood of responsibility for caring for elderly spouses is difficult to gauge. Women in general marry men who are older than themselves but the age differences are not on average very great. It would seem likely that the greater the age disparity between the spouses, the greater the likelihood of becoming a carer. It is interesting, then, to note the way in which family trends are changing. There has been a 400 per cent increase in the divorce rate in the last twenty years and this is linked to the increasing proportion of marriages which involve remarriage. At the present time more than one in three marriages involves remarriage for one or other spouse and some interesting differences emerge between the age distribution of spouses at first marriage and at second marriage.

Some evidence has become available about this topic from the 'record linkage' study of divorcees (Leete and Anthony, 1979). About the same proportion of men (75 per cent) married younger wives on both occasions—that is, first and second marriages—but 56 per cent of second wives were more than four years younger than their husbands compared with 25 per cent on the first occasion. At the extreme, for husbands, 2 per cent of first wives but 23 per cent of second wives were ten or *more* years younger than themselves. In contrast only 6 per cent of the wives in the sample (re)married people who were ten or more years their junior, and 10 per cent (re)married those who were ten or more years older. Such trends can therefore have important implications for the duration of widow(er)hood and for the probability that wives will have to care for their elderly husbands when they themselves are becoming frail. The pattern of remarriage is therefore making it more likely that women will be caught in the third part of the caring cycle.

Changing patterns

We have suggested both that the economic and financial loss to the carer has been underestimated partly because of the focus on the short term loss of income from employment and second, because little account is being taken of the possibility that women will experience more than one period of caring. It is also important to highlight the implications of the way in which employment patterns are changing. The view that married women might be at home in any event, has been refuted, earlier in the paper, by evidence of the importance of wives' earnings. There is also more direct evidence about married women's economic activity. Nearly 70 per cent of married women aged between 35 and 54 are economically active, that is, in work or seeking work (OPCS, 1981a, table 5.5, p. 83). A substantial minority of married women currently work part-time, some 40 per cent overall, and are often enabled by doing so to combine paid employment with home and family responsibilities.

But this picture of married women's participation is inadequate in a number of important respects (Rimmer and Popay, 1982). Firstly, this cross sectional picture of women's employment behaviour does not necessarily represent either the experience of an individual, or the experience of a cohort of women over time. Thus while only 55 per cent of married women aged between 55 and 59 are economically active today, one can envisage much higher levels of participation when today's 20-year-olds reach these age-groups. The difference in employment experience between today's 'middle-aged carers' and the younger women who are 'at risk' of being the carers in the future, is not easily quantifiable. But there is some evidence on the likely trends (Joshi and Owen, 1981, p. 22). Even over the 1970s there has been a substantial increase in the proportion of married women in all age-groups who are economically active. In 1971 46 per cent of married women aged between 25 and 44, and 53 per cent of those aged between 45 and 59 were economically active. In 1979 the figures were respectively 58 per cent and 61 per cent (Department of Employment, 1980, table 3, p. 3). Married women in all age-groups (except the oldest age-group) are now more likely to work than previously and it can be shown that younger cohorts are likely to spend a greater part of their lives economically active. Joshi and Owen, for example, show that cohorts of women reaching 60 in the 1950s had spent less than 40 per cent of their adult

lives at work as employees. A projection for those born half
a century later is, *ceteris paribus*, 60 per cent (Joshi and
Owen, 1981, p. 108). More tentatively, it might be suggested
that since women may in the future have a greater labour
force attachment than previously, they will be less likely to
consider undertaking part-time employment on a long-term
basis. This is particularly difficult to predict since there are
a number of countervailing factors, but it cannot be assumed
that the young women of today will be as readily available to
care as are those currently caring.

The true costs of community care

In future, then, it will not be acceptable to count as 'costless'
the input of informal carers—the majority of whom are
women and the majority of whom would be in paid employment, or in full-time employment rather than part-time
employment, if it were not for their caring role. It is clear
that the demands for care will increase. The Economist
Intelligence Unit estimated in 1976 that there would be an
increase annually of 0.9 per cent in the numbers of severely
disabled people, an increase of some 5,000 or so a year
(Economist Intelligence Unit 1976, quoted in EOC 1982a,
p. 5). Rossiter and Wicks have estimated that there will be
an extra 470,000 very dependent people (either housebound
or bedfast) in need of assistance by 2001 (Rossiter and
Wicks, 1982, p. 78).

It is also clear that if the present philosophy of shifting the
burden of care from the state back to the family is maintained,
women will suffer disproportionately. Many of the require-
ments for a more sexually egalitarian community care policy
have been set out by the EOC (EOC, 1982a, 1982b). But
what would a more adequate community care policy, which
reflected the costs to the carer, actually cost? Any attempt to
estimate additional resource costs of full recognition of the
contribution of women as informal carers must of necessity
be very tentative.

There are a number of approaches which could be adopted.
Some current estimates focus on the cost of extending existing

benefits—such as Invalid Care Allowance and Housewives Non-Contributory Invalidity Pension—to currently excluded groups. Estimates for extending Invalid Care Allowance range from £36 million at November 1979 benefit rates, to over £100 million two years later (EOC, 1981, p. 3). The net cost has more recently been estimated at £40 million. In addition, removal of the Household Duties Test on Housewives Non-Contributory Invalidity Pension was estimated to cost £168 million at July 1980 prices (NIAC, 1980, quoted in EOC, 1981, p. 4). Adding these two together would make extension of existing benefits as an option, cost between £200 million and £300 million. A more generous option, which involved increasing ICA and HNCIP to the long-term supplementary benefit rate might cost some £400 million, at 1981 prices. It is clear that the 'guestimates' on this basis can be no substitute for an adequately costed set of policy options. But the lack of such costings has been a prominent feature of the debate about the financial support of carers and stems from a more fundamental lack of knowledge about the true number of carers and their situation. This deficiency must be remedied before the debate can move on.

Looking to the future

It is inevitable that more public resources will need to be devoted to community care. The shifting age balance within the elderly population alone will, if the current level of services is maintained, require significant additional expenditure. Health and personal social services expenditure on persons over 75 is *seven times* higher than that on a person of working age and more significantly in this context over two and a half times as much as on a person aged 65–74 (The Treasury, 1982, table 2.11.10, p. 46). And it has been emphasised that existing public expenditure costs of care are kept low by ignoring the contribution of informal carers. It is particularly difficult to be certain about trends in employment, and whether these will disproportionately affect the real, as opposed to the theoretical, opportunity costs of employment for women. How long will the current high levels of unemployment exist, and what will this do to women's employment prospects? Similarly, it is difficult to know how changing family patterns will affect the willingness and availability of women to care. Increasing marriage breakdown may weaken family ties, or alternatively, make it easier for parents to move in to live with their divorced children (Rossiter and Wicks, 1982, p. 64). More work needs to be done on these questions, but there is no doubt that what is required is a fundamental shift in attitudes. The whole notion of community care needs to be reassessed to embrace the expectation that men, as well as women, will share in the responsibility of caring for others. Only in this way will there be less chance of women being disadvantaged—both as carers and as dependants--than they are now.

CHAPTER 8

Natural selection: perspectives on entitlement to the invalid care allowance

Dulcie Groves and Janet Finch

Introduction

Our aim in this paper is to offer a critique of the operation of entitlement to the invalid care allowance, a benefit which provides a particularly interesting example of the continuing differential treatment of men and women within the British social security system.

The ICA, a non-contributory cash payment (1982 value: £17.75 per week plus dependants' allowances)[1] was introduced by the Labour government in 1975. It is available to all men and to certain limited categories of women who have given up full-time paid work, in order to look after a severely disabled person (Rowland, ed., 1981, pp. 65–7). Initially the disabled person had to be a close relative, but from June 1981, availability was extended to those who care for more distant relatives and for friends. These changes did not, however, alter the ruling whereby married and cohabiting women cannot claim this benefit, even if they have given up paid work to care for a sick person. Separated, divorced and widowed women are likewise excluded if they are receiving maintenance allowances or pensions equivalent in value to ICA.

In the context of other discussions developed in this volume about women, work and caring, our interest in the ICA is two-fold. Firstly, it is the only state benefit which recognises the financial relationship between paid work and unpaid caring. The actual economic costs of giving up work in order to provide care (cf. Rimmer, in this volume) can be calculated in a variety of ways. ICA is noteworthy as providing the only mechanism whereby state policies acknowledge such costs and offer a very small gesture in mitigation of their effects, via an element of replacement-earnings for the carer.

Secondly, because rights of entitlement to this benefit do vary between women and men, and between different categories of women on grounds of marital status, the ICA offers an interesting instance of the way in which gender divisions operate in framing the rules of access to statutory welfare provision. The consequence of the operation of these rules is that such gender divisions are further reinforced, with the result that state policies have the effect of *shaping* social life and social relations, and not merely reflecting them (cf. Ungerson's and Walker's chapters in this volume). Thus the ICA can be viewed as a case-study of how state policies support and promote gender-related patterns of caring for the adult sick and disabled, and a crucial question can be raised as to whose interests are being served by the continuation of such patterns.

The development of the invalid care allowance

The invalid care allowance is available to men and to certain categories of unmarried women who have given up full-time paid employment (or, unusually, who have never done paid work) because they are caring at home for a severely disabled relative or friend. It is a condition of eligibility that the disabled person must be in receipt of the attendance allowance[2] (Rowland, 1981, pp. 102-6), which is not itself payable until the disability has lasted for six months. The disabled person must be cared for for at least 35 hours per week, with some provision for temporary breaks in caring. The carer must not be 'gainfully employed', that is in receipt of earnings in excess of £6 per week, discounting certain allowable employment expenses (Rowland, 1981, pp. 119-20). ICA is not means-tested, but is taxable except for any dependent child's allowance. It carries with it entitlement to credit for Class I social security contributions (Rowland, 1981, pp. 141-2). Recipients can, if deemed eligible, receive supplementary benefits in addition to the invalid care allowance (Allbeson, 1981, p. 5).

When the invalid care allowance was introduced in 1975, the target beneficiary was the single woman who had given up her job in order to care for an elderly parent (Hansard (Commons), cols 562-3, 29 January 1975). The financial needs of such women were publicised in the early 1960s by the Rev. Mary Webster.[3] She founded the National Council for the Single Woman and Her Dependants (1964) which aimed to advise and support single women 'carers' and to campaign on their behalf. An early victory was the introduction of the provision whereby single women carers who were eligible for National Assistance benefits could be credited with Class III National Insurance stamps so as to safeguard their statutory pension rights. In 1974 the White Paper on Social Security Provision for Chronically Sick and Disabled People (1974) proposed the introduction of a more widely available invalid care allowance 'for those of working age who would be breadwinners but for the need to stay at home and act as unpaid attendants to people who are severely disabled and need care' (House of Commons, 1974, §60, p. 19). Furthermore, the White Paper suggested the inclusion not only of relatives but also of 'long-standing members of the household'. However, married women and certain categories of unmarried women (likewise not deemed to be 'breadwinners') were to be excluded. In the debates at the time ICA was introduced, the claims of caring friends, not necessarily resident with the disabled person, were pressed. However, it was decided to confine the entitlement, in the first instance, to close relatives and step-relatives, with a promise to extend the allowance later to 'the equally deserving case of non-relatives' (Hansard (Commons), col. 643, 12 March 1975).

It has been estimated that there were 4,468 claimants during the first year of the invalid care allowance provision. This number had risen to 6,439 by the end of 1979.[4] The gross cost of the scheme in 1979 was estimated at £4 million (Hansard (Commons), 8 March 1979). However it appears that the original target group of single women constituted, in the event, less than one-third of all beneficiaries, with 1,700 'spinsters' out of a total of 6,100 in March 1979 (Hansard (Commons), 9 March 1979). These numbers were considerably less than the 11,500 anticipated in the 1974 White Paper on the basis of known numbers of claimants who had been receiving supplementary benefit 'for more than six months because they are looking after elderly or disabled relatives' (House of Commons, 1974, §61, p. 20). They are also less than the 13,000 claimants recorded by the Supplementary Benefits Commission in 1979 as those who 'were required at home to care for other adults and would thus normally qualify for invalid care allowance' (Supplementary Benefits Commission, 1980, §8.24, p. 67). Despite this, by March 1980 it was claimed that 'the original estimate was too high and there is now little practical difference between the number receiving the benefit and the number entitled to it' (Hansard (Commons), col. 629, 12 February 1980).

In June 1981 there were an estimated 6,450 ICA beneficiaries, at a cost of £8 million for 1981/82, including 3,300 'single' women (counting in widows) and 3,150 men. The government regretted that separate figures for single and married men were not available (Hansard (Commons), col. 100, 23 October 1981). These figures without doubt severely under-represent the total number of carers: they are likely to be far less than the numbers reliant for income on some sort of transfer payment (notably supplementary benefit) and certainly far less than the number of carers who incur financial loss by giving up paid work to care. It may be noted that in the first year of the scheme, 11,394 claims were rejected—a total of 71.7 per cent of all applicants. The majority of refusals were to married women or to persons who had reached 'pensionable age'.[5]

In the early days of the scheme, government concern was expressed at the apparent failure of large numbers of people to apply for ICA, despite publicity for the benefit (see for example, Hansard (Commons), col. 77, 12 July 1977). By 1980, however, as shown above, the government was arguing that all persons who were eligible for ICA were receiving it. It is true that in 1979 not one of the 97 appeals resulted in a decision in the claimant's favour (DHSS, 1980b, table 16.30, p. 92). However, this may owe more to the very explicit nature of the rules of entitlement than to a near-perfect take-up rate for this benefit. Furthermore, arguments which attempt to prove high take-up rates by those actually eligible for a particular benefit, do not deal with issues of non-eligibility for entitlement in the first place. Although eligibility for ICA was extended in June 1981 to those caring for distant kin and non-relatives (thereby bringing an estimated further 2,000 beneficiaries into the scheme), the rules of entitlement relating to the marital status of female claimants were retained.

Thus the new regulations have undoubtedly served to compound already existing inequities in the rules of entitlement. It is to these inequities, and the ideologies which govern their continuing existence, to which we now turn.

Entitlements, inequities and the 'natural selection' model

Our analysis of the inequities in the operation of ICA and the assumptions about 'caring' which they imply rests principally upon an examination of formal regulations.

It is clear that within the operations of the invalid care allowance scheme, significant variations occur in the operation of the rules about sex, marital status and, until 1981, kinship.[6] If one views the regulations from the standpoint of the carer these variations can be defined as inequities, because individuals providing essentially similar caring services do not have similar rights to claim the invalid care allowance. It was the clear intent of parliamentary legislators that some categories of individual should be favoured by being entitled to claim the allowance, while others are excluded from it. Thus, the exclusion of married and cohabiting women from entitlement to invalid care allowance rests on two fundamental assumptions about them: firstly, that women in general, and married women in particular, are the 'natural' carers in the domestic setting (Finch and Groves, 1980; Graham, in this volume); secondly, that married women's earnings, if any, are marginal to the financial security of the domestic group (see Land, 1977).

The exclusion of married women from entitlement on the grounds that they are the 'natural' carers at home is plainly demonstrated in the arguments of the 1974 White Paper where the proposal for the exclusion of married women is justified 'as they might be at home in any event' (House of Commons, 1974, §60, p. 20). The possibility of extending ICA to married women has been a recurrent issue ever since the allowance was introduced and the same rationale for their exclusion has continued to be given. For example, in an oral Parliamentary answer in 1975, a Minister of the Department of Health and Social Security replied that 'It will not be payable to married women in general because many such women have, in any event, reasons for staying at home which are not connected with the need to care for a severely disabled relative. For example, many married women remain at home to care for their young children: others have elderly parents who are not disabled living with them' (Hansard (Commons), col. 97, 4 November 1975). The then Labour government regarded it as too complex an exercise to identify a class of *married* women who would be in full-time work but for the need to care for a severely disabled relative (House of Commons, Official Report, Standing Committee B, vol. 3, col. 344, 14 January 1975). Rather than recognise married or cohabiting women as bona fide paid workers, the government preferred to exclude them as a category. Their exclusion is part of the process whereby social policies reinforce the presumed obligation of married women to perform unpaid domestic services for other members of their kin group (Land, 1978).

The fact that a married woman *can* (exceptionally) claim the allowance if she is separated from her husband, employed (but giving up work to care) and not being maintained by him (see Rowland, ed., 1981, p. 66) underlines the second reason for the exclusion of married women as a category. Married women are treated as financial dependants of their husbands and by definition as therefore not in need of, or entitled to, a benefit which is designed, essentially, to replace earnings.[7] Even if a married woman is not in paid employment because she is caring for an infirm person, it is assumed that the earnings which she has lost are marginal to her needs, since she derives her basic support from her dependence on her husband's earnings. Only where such financial dependency is demonstrably not applicable, can a married woman claim the invalid care allowance.

This line of thinking, apparent in the early days of the allowance, has been reiterated in the Department of Health and Social Security's comments on the report of the National Insurance Advisory Committee (NIAC, 1980) which was asked to consider the possibility of extending entitlement to the allowance. The Department argued that the allowance was 'an income maintenance benefit designed to replace, at least in part, the earnings derived income of those who, in general, had no other source of income. . . . Married and co-habiting women, on the other hand, had the support of their partner's income' (NIAC, 1980, §16, p. 6). By the same reasoning, women receiving maintenance from a former husband are, if they give up employment to care, similarly excluded from receipt of the allowance, unless their income is less than the amount of the invalid care allowance. Rules which prohibit receipt of 'overlapping' statutory benefits can prohibit widows from entitlement to ICA unless their state pension is less than the amount of ICA (Rowland, 1981, pp. 120-3). By contrast, occupational benefits, such as widows' pensions or early retirement superannuation, do not appear to affect entitlement to ICA for either men or women.

The invalid care allowance can be cited as a singularly clear example of the sex discrimination which the law continues to permit in the field of social security. There is no reason to suppose that any government will wish to rectify this anomaly of its own volition in the foreseeable future, since an extension of entitlement would be expensive, as well as conceding further legal rights to financial independence to married and cohabiting women. Even when the EEC directive on equal treatment for men and women in social security is applied to the British system, non-contributory benefits such as the invalid care allowance will not be affected (Atkins, 1981, p. 20).

As previously stated, the original target beneficiaries for the allowance were single women, primarily single daughters caring for elderly parents. As a government minister made clear in the Commons debate on the introduction of the benefit, 'It is important to accept that the group of people whom ICA was primarily designed to aid . . . were single women who devote their lives to looking after elderly parents or some other sick members of the family' (House of Commons Official Report, Standing Committee B, vol. 3, 14 January 1975). The reasons why the government succumbed to pressure to introduce a measure to aid single women in particular, are somewhat obscure. We can speculate that part of the explanation may have lain in the growing scarcity value of that vanishing species—the middle-aged single daughter. A familiar phenomenon of the inter-war period, her single state attributed to the heavy loss of male life in the First World War, the 'spinster' had become less common by the mid-1960s, and even more of a rarity by the mid-1970s.[8] On the pages of Hansard she appears as a stereotyped figure calculated to excite both pity and patronage, with unpaid domestic labour in the parental home viewed as a poor alternative to a similar 'career' in the matrimonial home (see Hansard (Commons), col. 1609, 21 November 1974).

Single women were viewed as one small supply of rather cheap care for the severely disabled and the 1974–9 Labour government, like its Conservative successor, regarded it as entirely appropriate, indeed commendable, that single daughters should give up work so as to provide this care, despite the warning of the 1974 White Paper that a 'long period of caring for a sick relative may mean that the "attendant" emerges at the end with poor health and poor prospects of getting a job' (House of Commons, 1974, §42, p. 13).

Such sacrificial action was apparently regarded as a demonstration of filial 'devotion' shown by daughters and (rather less frequently) by sons. This is particularly well illustrated in the following extract from a back-bencher's speech:

> Many lasses, and the occasional lads, have sacrificed career and prospects of marriage, to demonstrate their devotion to handicapped relatives. The ICA will bring a gleam of light into what must be very drab lives particularly of those who have chosen, because of their own inherent decency, to be trapped into an existence of unpaid nurse and companion and have so long appeared to be neglected or forgotten. The allowance will be warmly welcomed by those people who lead lives of continual quiet despair and misery (Hansard (Commons), col. 1609, 21 November 1974).

In recompense for a life of quiet despair and misery, £17.75 a week sounds more like an insult than a gleam of light; but such sentiments conspicuously omit to question whether anyone should actually be placed in this situation from necessity, or even from choice, preferring to concentrate instead upon the moral worth of the carers.

However, what was considered sauce for the single goose was certainly not held to be appropriate for the married gander. The 1974 White Paper on its discussion of 'help for the disabled housewife' stated firmly that 'It is in the interests of society that the family should be kept together and that the breadwinner should not be forced to give up his job to do the domestic tasks which have become beyond his wife's capacity' (House of Commons, 1974, §65, p. 20). Thus, in the mid-1970s very different assumptions were made about the obligation of single daughters on the one hand and married men on the other. Married men were designated as wage earners, single women (and the occasional man) as carers whose loss of income merited a modest financial recompense, while married women were financially dependent and 'at home in any event'.

Assumptions about the special nature of kinship obligations are evident in the discussions preceding the extension of the invalid care allowance to non-relatives. Until June 1981, it was very much a benefit which kept caring within the family, though the possibility of making it available to non-related carers was a live issue right from the beginning. As such, it was much discussed preparatory to legislation and the Labour government's response was moderately sympathetic in that they promised that 'deserving cases of non-relatives will be brought into the ICA arrangements once we have got over the initial and major hurdle of paying the allowance to relatives . . .' (Hansard (Commons), col. 646, 12 March 1975). It is clear that cases where non-relatives provide care were regarded as especially 'deserving' in that such actions go beyond what are normally regarded as the obligations of friendship or neighbourliness, 'the act of the friend could be even more noble than that of the devoted daughter who has given up so much for so many years to look after a parent' (Hansard (Commons), col. 563, 29 January 1975). Thus was the case advanced for a financial reward for non-relatives who give up work to care. Kinship relations, however, would appear to entail the provision of caring services as of right by female kin whose 'natural' setting is the home, that is, married women. In such circumstances, as previously illustrated (p. 149 of this chapter), financial recompense or reward is viewed as much less appropriate, since the married woman is doing no more than fulfil her 'natural' obligations (Rose and Rose, 1982).

It is not surprising to find, therefore, that when the possibility of the extension of the benefit was eventually raised again, the group selected for special consideration was not married women but a specific group of non-relatives, namely, cohabiting men. The National Insurance Advisory Committee was asked to consider

> whether, and if so on what basis, there is any category for
> extending title to the Invalid Care Allowance . . . to any
> specific category of non-relatives and in particular whether
> priority should be given to cases in which a man claims in
> respect of the care he gives to an invalid woman with
> whom he is living as husband and wife (NIAC, 1980,
> §1, p. 3).

The Department of Health and Social Security's estimate was that there were 200–300 men in this situation and that the cost of extending ICA to them would be about £150,000 less savings on supplementary benefits previously paid to men (NIAC, 1980, §21, p. 7). This group of 'caring' men, about whom there was governmental concern, is minuscule by comparison with the likely number of 'caring' married women about whose financial circumstances there is no concern. Successive governments have steadfastly refused to consider the extension of ICA to married and cohabiting women, citing the high cost as a deterrent. In April 1982 the gross cost of extending ICA to all married women was estimated at £100 million, which gives some crude indication of the large numbers of married women carers who may currently be excluded from entitlement (Hansard (Commons), col. 433, 8 April 1982).

The National Insurance Advisory Committee's recommendation that ICA should *not* be extended specifically to cohabiting men rested not on a devaluation of their needs, but upon a recognition of the anomalies implicit in any attempt to distinguish between specific types of non-relative (NIAC, 1980, §25, p. 8). It may be noted that tests of cohabitation are no bar to the denial of entitlement to *women* attempting to claim social security benefits, not least under the ICA scheme itself.

In the event, the committee recommended the extension of ICA to 'people who are looking after non-relatives and to people looking after those relatives not covered by the present provisions' with no special priority for cohabiting men (NIAC, 1980, §28, p. 8). Married and cohabiting women were still to be excluded along with other 'dependent' women, applicants over pensionable age and persons in receipt of 'overlapping benefits'. The entitlement of married women to ICA had in fact been placed outside the remit of the question put to the National Insurance Advisory Committee, though, as will be noted later, this did not prevent the committee from commenting on this exclusion.

From 1 June 1981, therefore, the ICA became available to all non-relatives who met the criteria for entitlement, but not to married or cohabiting women (Hansard (Commons), cols 78-9, 6 May 1981). There now exists the interesting anomaly that a woman can claim ICA if she cares for a lover who happens to be female, but not for one who happens to be male. We wonder whether it was the intention of the Department of Health and Social Security to encourage this particular model of family life.

In summary, this examination of the implications of variations in entitlement to ICA demonstrates that until recently the rationale for the particular patterns of entitlement to invalid care allowance rested upon what we are calling the 'natural selection' mode of inter-personal obligations. The benefit is a 'selective' one, not in the traditional sense of being means-tested, but in the sense that it is available to 'selected' persons who provide care in a particular context defined by their relationship to the 'cared-for' person. The benefit was originally provided for those who 'naturally' could be expected to provide care (such as close blood-relatives) and subsequently to those such as friends and neighbours who are 'naturally' regarded as giving care beyond the call of duty if they actually give up their paid employment so as to care. By the same token, the invalid care allowance is 'naturally' not available to married women, who surely can be expected to provide care without any necessity for recompense when paid work is given up.

The invalid care allowance and state social policy

The invalid care allowance, whilst on one level representing a single and discrete piece of social policy, cannot simply be seen as an individual item of policy-making, designed to meet a specific need without reference to other provision. The ICA is one of a range of benefits through which the state intervenes in domestic relationships in such a way as to reinforce the presumed financial dependency of women (especially in marriage) within a specific form of family organisation. The idea that the marriage contract entails entering into that kind of dependency relationship is so strong that (in the case of ICA as with other benefits) it is extended to unmarried women who can be deemed to be living in a 'marriage-like' relationship. This structure of dependency is tied closely to the notion that the male wage is a family wage (Land, 1980; McIntosh, 1981). If ICA is part of a particular pattern in state interventions in domestic relationships (cf. Ungerson, in this volume) then a set of linked questions are raised: why are such interventions made and to what end; what, in practice, are their consequences; and what is the particular position of the ICA within these processes? The most general issues cannot be dealt with fully here; but by looking at them through the particular instance of ICA, some hitherto underemphasised issues are illuminated.

Under the influence of recent important developments in both Marxist and feminist analyses of state policies, the role of state welfare in shaping and sustaining a particular family form is often presented as part of both representing and promoting the needs of a capitalist economy. In its most crude version, the account runs like this. The state maintains a family form in which a man and a woman plus their dependent children constitute a separate household. Within that unit, the man is the wage worker and the woman the domestic worker and the whole unit depends upon the man's wage for survival. This family form serves the needs of capital very well; firstly, because it reproduces the labour power of the present and the next generation of wage labourers at very low cost to capital; and secondly, because it maintains women as a reserve army of labour, to be drawn in and out of the labour market as the needs of capital dictate. At the same time, the interests of men are also served by processes which sustain patriarchal patterns of gender domination. Any 'welfare' measures which sustain this family form are ultimately in the interests of capital, although usually they are presented as being for the benefit of those who receive them. This account is powerful in unmasking other versions of social policy, presented uncritically as the actions of a benevolent state on behalf of its less advantaged citizens. It has a clear applicability to benefits like ICA, which 'reward' certain types of 'family' activity, when undertaken by 'spinsters' or men, while requiring married women to undertake the same activities without explicit financial recompense. It is, however, an account which is clearly too simple. It can be criticised at the theoretical level for presenting a rather naive, functionalist account of the relationship between the state and the economy. It can also be criticised at the empirical level, when it does not fully account for particular instances of social policy. How far does the example of ICA fit this kind of account? Conversely, where does the account have to be modified to accommodate the issues raised by ICA?

Essentially, the case of ICA does not easily support the view that social policy should be viewed as a single-minded action on the part of government designed to advance the interests of capitalist employers. In this instance, it looks much more like the product of a situation in which governments were pursuing different interlocking (but not always entirely compatible) policy agendas. In terms of its outcomes (whether intended or unintended) it is not entirely clear who should be counted as the real beneficiaries of this policy. Certainly it is not unambiguously in the interests of capital in the short (or even the longer) term. This view of the ICA can be supported by looking briefly at three aspects of its development and operation, as presented in this chapter: firstly, by considering those aspects of ICA which can be seen as a concession and even as a gain for its recipients; second, by relating the argument about sustaining a particular family form to the categories of elderly and handicapped; and thirdly, by examining the relationship between ICA and the search for low-cost solutions in social service provision.

Firstly, the ICA quite clearly was introduced as a result of pressure-group activity by people claiming to represent the interests of single women carers. There must therefore be a prima facie case for seeing it as an instance of a welfare measure which is a concession won *from* the state, rather than a measure imposed *by* the state (Gough, 1979, pp. 64–5; McIntosh, 1981, pp. 35–6). Without doubt the introduction of ICA represents a positive (if very limited) gain for those individuals who do receive it. Clearly it is better to receive *some* financial support for caring than none at all; and the granting of this benefit does afford some measure of public recognition that, behind the rather sentimental rhetoric of 'care', the task of looking after a handicapped person entails necessarily very demanding *work* (Parker, 1981; Graham, in this volume). Further, the gains would be very real in both material and ideological terms if this benefit were to be extended to those women who currently are not entitled to receive it. Quite apart from a slight improvement in their financial position, it would represent an important ideological victory, since it would be a recognition within public policy that married and other allegedly 'dependent' women are properly entitled to some payment for the domestic services which they perform.

The gains (both actual and potential) are not entirely unambiguous however. The prospect of the benefit's being extended to married women raises again all the dilemmas of the wages-for-housework debate.[9] In the short term, the financial position of certain women carers may be eased; but in the long term, the price is that women's position as the allegedly 'natural' carers in the family may be reinforced. Even the gains of the benefit as it presently operates cannot be regarded as unambiguous. In so far as it makes it slightly more possible to keep caring for elderly and handicapped dependants within the household, the ICA reinforces the processes whereby the needs of such individuals are treated as a private rather than a public issue. The strengthening of the family or household as the location where it appears 'natural' for such caring to take place may indeed be in the long-term interests of capital. The fact that some gains are made by groups of citizens—in this case male and single women carers —does not mean that the measures introduced cannot also be serving other interests.

The second aspect of the ICA, which opens up some interesting issues about state welfare and the family, is the question of how the elderly and handicapped fit into the above account of the sustaining of the nuclear family form in the interests of capital. On the whole, they fit rather badly. If the state's interest in maintaining the nuclear family-household form is to secure the reproduction of the working class, then it is by no means clear how the elderly and handicapped are part of that process. Non-handicapped children are the future generation of wage labourers, adult males are the present generation, adult women are the reserve army. What are the sick and handicapped? Purely from this viewpoint of reproducing labour power, it is not clear why the state (acting, on this argument, in the interests of capital) should be interested in supporting them at all, except as some part of very generalised activity of reproducing the working class (Gough, 1979, p. 45; McIntosh, 1979, p. 169).

It seems that the adult handicapped are a group where the account of state interventions in the family fits rather badly. Perhaps more interestingly, they may also be a group whose position in the underlying processes is inherently ambiguous. The logic that (from that point of view of capital) they are useless and therefore might as well be allowed to die off is presumably a logic which an overtly liberal and democratic state is not able to pursue. It does, however, help to explain why (as will be argued shortly) they are a group in relation to whose care the idea of low-cost, 'community' services have been particularly promoted. Since the returns for investment in this group are virtually nil from the viewpoint of capital, they need to be catered for at minimum cost. Given that the nuclear family–household form is being supported on other grounds, it seems to offer a neat solution to the care of this apparently useless group. The idea of women as the natural carers can easily be promoted in this context, since it merely entails an extension of their designated roles as unpaid providers of child care in the home and 'servicers' of adult males (see Graham, this volume).

However, the family form thus promoted does not always perform very efficiently those tasks which the state (in whoever's interests it is acting) would like to assign it. One important reason why it cannot work very well is that not all elderly people have relatives or friends who can potentially be designated as their carers and/or their financial supporters. As McIntosh has argued, 'Old age and the disablement of men are the two situations where the state has to some extent recognised the needs unmet by the wage system and allowed the principle of individual dependence upon the state, regardless of household circumstances' (McIntosh, 1978, p. 273). In practice such provision is very much residual, that is, offered as a last resort. But the very fact that direct dependence on the state is acknowledged in some circumstances indicates that the argument about the state's support of the needs of capital through the family wage system needs to be modified to take account of the social and economic circumstances of all citizens, and not just healthy adults and their young children.

Thirdly, the ICA has to be seen as part of a wider endeavour, evident from the mid-1970s onwards, to search out low-cost solutions in the field of welfare provision, in the wake of public expenditure cuts. This can be seen, as a number of writers have noted, as a process of restructuring welfare so that some former gains are eroded, and the state withdraws from many areas of provision, leaving various forms of commercial, voluntary and privatised provision to fill the gap (Gough, 1979, ch. 7). In the case of the elderly and handicapped, the notion of community care has been in the forefront of rhetoric about low-cost solutions (Finch and Groves, 1980), and the ICA obviously is a measure which appears to offer some kind of incentive for people to care for their handicapped relatives in their own homes—or at least make it more *possible* for them to do so. From the point of view of public expenditure, the money spent on ICA is a small price to pay for keeping people out of expensive residential institutions which probably are the only viable alternative for most of them.

Thus the ICA is an example of a piece of social policy which, whilst its origins can be traced to political demands (in this case to concessions gained by a disadvantaged group), once established can be used for rather different ends. The extension of ICA to non-relatives six years after its introduction can be seen as a decision related to the extension of low-cost community care policies, rather than to any kind of response to demands from potential beneficiaries. Once established, the ICA offered a tempting means of encouraging more people to care for the handicapped and elderly outside the framework of state-provided services.

Does this mean that it is inevitable that the benefit will eventually be extended to married women, since they provide an attractive large pool of people who might be persuaded to care for their handicapped and elderly relatives in greater numbers? Here we encounter an interesting dilemma, in which two different agendas which state policies might pursue appear incompatible. Pressure to keep down the costs of publicly provided services may begin to make it look very attractive to extend the ICA to married women. But in the long term, such a move might seriously undermine the maintenance of the patriarchal form of the nuclear family–household, by cutting across the principle of married women's financial dependence and acknowledging that some element of pay for work done in the home is appropriate.

Conclusion

This chapter has concentrated specifically upon entitlement to the invalid care allowance, a focus which has allowed us to highlight a number of issues which are central to the theme of women, work and caring. We have argued that ICA is a benefit which plainly slots into a gender-specific pattern of welfare provision, a system which serves to maintain traditional patterns of gender domination. In the case of the invalid care allowance, this happens both directly and indirectly. Because the rules of entitlement discriminate between potential clients on grounds of both gender and marital status, ICA is a provision which directly reinforces the subordinate and dependent position of women. More indirectly, it is part of a range of benefits which serve to support a particular family form which is itself patriarchal.

Prominent among such provisions is supplementary benefit, a means-tested cash allowance which constitutes the only source of financial support for some carers who are not entitled to ICA. For others, it literally supplements ICA. Like ICA, it is not currently available to married and cohabiting women. The limitations of both ICA and supplementary benefits as basic income support for carers, have led some commentators to begin exploration of alternative modes of financial assistance for those who give up paid work to care. These range from a carer's benefit analogous to child benefit (EOC, 1982b, pp. 26–7), inclusion of a contributory carers' benefit in the national insurance scheme (NCSWD, 1982) through to tax reforms which advocate diversion of the married man's tax allowance, in part, to provide financial assistance for carers (Lister, 1980, pp. 145–6). The Equal Opportunities Commission strongly advocates extension of ICA to all women and its payment at a rate equivalent to long-term supplementary benefit (EOC, 1982b, pp. 26–7).

The introduction of ICA was a real gain for such limited categories of carers who became entitled to it. A further extension to all women (particularly if accompanied by an increase in its cash value and the inclusion of beneficiaries caring for incapacitated people not qualified for receipt of attendance allowance), would equally represent real gain. However, the interests of certain other groups are better served by a restructured system of income support for carers, such as we have now, which keeps down public expenditure costs and is designed to maintain the nuclear family as a 'caring' unit. Such groups can be variously seen as the wealthy who will benefit if taxes are cut, as capitalists who can use the family for the reproduction of labour power or as men, for whom this family form represents a crucial means of maintaining the gender order. Whatever the balance of gains for each of these groups (and the issues are complex, as has been demonstrated) we argue that the rules of establishment upon which provision of the invalid care allowance *currently* operates, make it a benefit which is not in the collective long-term interests of women.[10]

Notes

Chapter 2 Why do women care?

1 This chapter arises out of work commissioned and funded by the
SSRC and submitted to them in a report entitled *Women, work and
the 'caring capacity of the community: a report of a research review'.*
I am grateful to the SSRC for the grant which enabled me to do this
work and for their permission to reproduce some of the report here.

Chapter 3 Employment, women and their disabled children

1 At the height of the thalidomide crisis in 1972, the government
established a discretionary fund to help families with severely
disabled children, to be administered by the Joseph Rowntree
Memorial Trust. The Trust also established a research project at the
University of York to evaluate the Family Fund and to investigate
the more general problems arising out of severe disablement in
children. See Bradshaw (1980).

Chapter 4 The caring wife

1 I acknowledge with deep gratitude the support, both financial and
moral, of the King's Fund Centre and the Equal Opportunities
Commission which enabled these interviews to take place and the
Association of Carers to be established.
2 Mobility allowance is a taxable cash benefit, 1981-2 value £16.50
per week for people who are unable to walk (see Rowland, ed., 1981,
pp. 96-102).
3 Attendance allowance is a non-taxable cash benefit, 1981-82 value
£23.65 (higher rate) or £15.75 (lower rate) payable to people who
have been so severely disabled for at least six months that they
require attention or supervision by day and night (for higher rate)
or by day or by night (for lower rate) (ibid., pp. 102-6).

4 The post-war national insurance legislation derived from the ideologies of the Beveridge Report (Cmd 6404 (1942), Social Insurance and Allied Services, London, HMSO) in which married women were clearly defined as housewives, financially dependent on their husbands.

5 The main method which the groups use to recruit members is the local press and radio, and this seems to work fairly well, especially when the speaker or interviewee is a carer herself.

Chapter 5 Single carers: employment, housework and caring

1 The study was supported by the Social Science Research Council through a post-graduate studentship and by a Marjorie Warren award.

2 At the insistence of the area health authority prior appointments were made with the respondents. The non-response rate for men was 40 per cent and for women 29 per cent. Although this seems high, it compared favourably with similar studies. George and Wilding had a non-response rate of 38 per cent in a study of motherless families. A contracting out letter was used to approach the fathers (George and Wilding, 1972, p. 15). Marsden had a somewhat higher non-response rate of 44 per cent when writing to a sample of mothers dependent on supplementary benefit to request an interview (Marsden, 1973, p. 340).

Chapter 8 Natural selection: perspectives on entitlement to the invalid care allowance

1 An increase of £10.65 per week is payable for an adult dependant and £7.70 for a child dependant.

2 Invalid care allowance is granted to a 'carer' *only* when the disabled person being cared for is eligible for the attendance allowance. There is evidence that entitlement to the attendance allowance may sometimes operate inequitably, since it rests on tests of incapacity which are themselves problematic (Bradshaw and Lawton, 1980). Such inequities must mean that there are some carers who are not receiving the invalid care allowance while being in apparently similar circumstances to others who do. This factor goes some way towards explaining the discrepancy between estimated and actual claims for ICA referred to previously.

3 Verbal communication: Heather McKenzie (Director) and Margaret Lofthouse (Development Officer), National Council for the Single Woman and Her Dependants.

4 Personal communication: D. Welsh, Statistics and Research Branch, DHSS, Central Office, Newcastle-upon-Tyne, 19 September 1980.

5 60 for women, 65 for men (Rowland, ed., 1981, p. 74).

6 'Close relatives' were defined as: great grandparent, grandparent,

parent, child, grandchild, great grandchild, husband, wife, step-parent, step-child, brother, sister, half-brother, half-sister, step-sister, step-brother, aunt, uncle, nephew, niece, father-in-law, mother-in-law, brother-in-law, sister-in-law, son-in-law or daughter-in-law (Rowland, 1981, p. 50).

7   For a discussion of the legal obligation of husbands to maintain wives see O'Donovan, in Burman, ed., 1979, pp. 134–52. O'Donovan argues that 'the husband's maintenance obligation is the explanation offered for refusal of financial benefits to the wife in a number of situations, yet in legal practice that obligation means very little' (p. 141).

8   Taking women of 40–44, 18 per cent were 'spinsters' in 1931, 14 per cent in 1951, 10 per cent in 1961, 7 per cent in 1971, 6 per cent in 1975 and 1979. In 1951 there were 238,000 single women in this age-group, compared with 76,000 by 1979, England and Wales (OPCS, 1981b, tables 1.1a and b, pp. 15, 17).

9   For a discussion of 'wages for housework' see Malos, 1980.

10 In late June 1982, the Secretary of State for Social Services was reported (*Guardian*, 29 June 1982) to be considering as a priority the 'extension' of benefits to help people 'caring' at home for the handicapped, sick and elderly. In the light of our analysis, it will indeed be interesting to see what form this 'extension' will take.

Bibliography

Adams, C.T. and Winston, K.T. (1980), *Mothers at Work*, London, Longman.

Adams, M. (1971), 'The compassion trap' in Gornick, V. and Moran, B.K. (eds), *Women in Sexist Society*, New York, Basic Books.

Age Concern (1982), *Caring for the Carers*, Mitcham, Surrey, Age Concern.

Allbeson, J. (ed.) (1981), *National Welfare Benefits Handbook*, eleventh edition, London, Child Poverty Action Group.

Anderson, M. (1977), 'The impact upon family relationships of the elderly of changes since Victorian times in government income maintenance provision', in Shanas, E. and Sussman, M. (eds), *Family, Bureaucracy and the Elderly*, Durham, North Carolina, Duke University Press.

Atkins, S. (1981), 'Social Security Act 1980 and the EEC Directive on Equal Treatment in Social Security Benefits', *Journal of Social Welfare Law*, January, pp. 16-20.

Baker Miller, J. (1976), *Towards a New Psychology of Women*, Harmondsworth, Middlesex, Penguin Books.

Baldock, J. and Prior, D. (1981), 'Social workers talking to clients: a study of verbal behaviour', *British Journal of Social Work*, vol. 11, pp. 19-38.

Baldwin, S. (1976a), *Disabled Children: Counting the Costs*, London, Disability Alliance.

Baldwin, S. (1976b), 'Families with handicapped children', in Jones, K. (ed.), *The Yearbook of Social Policy in Britain 1975*, London, Routledge & Kegan Paul.

Baldwin, S. (1981), 'The financial consequences of disablement in children', unpublished research report, University of York, Social Policy Research Unit.

Barclay, P.M. (Chairman) (1982), *Social Workers: Their Role and Tasks*, Report of a Working Party set up in October 1980, at the request of the Secretary of State for Social Services, by the National Institute for Social Work, London, Bedford Square Press of the National Council for Voluntary Organisations.

Barrett, M. (1980), *Women's Oppression Today: Problems in Marxist Feminist Analysis*, London, Verso Editions and NLB.

Bayley, M. (1973), *Mental Handicap and Community Care*, London, Routledge & Kegan Paul.

Bebbington, A.C. (1980), 'Changes in the provision of social services to the elderly in the community over fourteen years', *Social Policy and Administration*, vol. 13, no. 2, pp. 114–23.

Bebbington, A.C. (1981), 'Appendix', in Goldberg, E.M. and Hatch, S. (eds) (1981).

Beveridge, W. (1942), *Social Insurance and Allied Services*, Cmd 6404, London, HMSO.

Blaxter, M. (1976), *The Meaning of Disability*, London, Heinemann.

Boston Women's Health Book Collective (1971), *Our Bodies, Our Selves*, New York, Simon & Schuster.

Bowlby, J. (1963), *Child Care and the Growth of Love*, Harmondsworth, Penguin Books.

Bradshaw, J. (1975), *The Financial Needs of Disabled Children*, London, Disability Alliance.

Bradshaw, J. (1980), *The Family Fund: an Initiative in Social Policy*, London, Routledge & Kegan Paul.

Bradshaw, J. and Lawton, D. (1980), 'An examination of equity in the administration of the attendance allowance', *Policy and Politics*, vol. 8, no. 1, pp. 39–54.

Breugel, I. (1979), 'Women as a reserve army of labour: a note on recent British experience', *The Feminist Review 3*, pp. 12–23.

Breugel, I. (1978), 'What keeps the family going?', *International Socialism*, vol. 2, no. 1, pp. 2–15.

Briggs, A. (1981), 'Who cares? Report of a door-to-door survey of people caring for dependent relatives', privately produced paper, Whitley Bay.

Bristow, A. (1981), *Crossroads Care Attendant Schemes*, Rugby, Association of Crossroads Care Attendant Schemes.

British Association of Social Workers (1982), *Services for Elderly People*, Birmingham, BASW.

Burman, S. (ed.) (1979), *Fit Work for Women*, London, Croom Helm.

Burton, L. (1975), *The Family Life of Sick Children*, London, Routledge & Kegan Paul.

Butcher, H. and Crosbie, D. (1978). *Pensioned Off*, York, University of York/Cumbria Community Development Project.

Butler, N. (ed.) (1976), *Housing Problems of Handicapped People in Bristol*, Child Health Research Unit, University of Bristol.

Byrne, P.S. and Long, B.E.L. (1976), *Doctors Talking to Patients: a Study of the Verbal Behaviour of General Practitioners Consulting in their Surgeries*, London, HMSO.

Cartwright, A., Hockey, L. and Anderson, J. (1973), *Life Before Death*, London, Routledge & Kegan Paul.

Central Statistical Office (1979), *Social Trends 10*, 1980 edition, London, HMSO.

Central Statistical Office (1980), *Social Trends 11*, 1981 edition,
London, HMSO.

Central Statistical Office (1981), *Social Trends 12*, 1982 edition,
London, HMSO.

Challis, D. and Davies, B. (1980), 'A new approach to community care
for the elderly', *British Journal of Social Work*, vol. 10, no. 1,
pp. 1-18.

Chodorow, N. (1971), 'Being and doing' in Gornick, V. and Moran,
B.K. (eds), *Women in Sexist Society*, New York, Basic Books.

Chodorow, N. (1978), *The Reproduction of Mothering*, London,
University of California Press.

Counter Information Services (1981), *Women in the 1980s*, London,
CIS.

Coussins, J. and Coote, A. (1981), *The Family in the Firing Line*,
London, National Council for Civil Liberties/Child Poverty Action
Group.

Dahl, T.S. and Snare, A. (1978), 'The coercion of privacy', in Smart, C.
and Smart, B., *Women, Sexuality and Social Control*, London,
Routledge & Kegan Paul.

Dartington, T. (1980), *Family Care of Old People*, London, Souvenir
Press.

De Beauvoir, S. (1972), *The Second Sex*, Harmondsworth, Penguin
Books.

Deeping, E. (1979), *Caring for Elderly Parents*, London, Constable.

Department of Employment (1975), *Women and Work: a Review*,
Manpower Paper No. 11, London, HMSO.

Department of Employment (1980), *Background Paper to the Green
Paper on the Taxation of Husband and Wife*, London, Department
of Employment.

Department of Employment (1982), *Family Expenditure Survey 1980*,
London, HMSO.

Department of Health and Social Security (1976), *Priorities for Health
and Personal Social Services in England*, London, HMSO.

Department of Health and Social Security (1978), *A Happier Old Age*,
London, HMSO.

Department of Health and Social Security (1980a), *Social Security Act
1980*, London, HMSO.

Department of Health and Social Security (1980b), *Social Security
Statistics 1980 (Incorporating 1979)*, London, HMSO.

Department of Health and Social Security (1981a), *Care in Action; a
Handbook of Policies and Priorities for the Health and Social
Services in England*, London, HMSO.

Department of Health and Social Security (1981b), *Care in the Community: A Consultative Document on Moving Resources for Care in
England*, London, DHSS.

Department of Health and Social Security (1981c), *Growing Older*,
Cmnd 8173, London, HMSO.

Department of Health and Social Security (1981d), *Report on a Study of Community Care*, London, HMSO.

Derow, E. (1981), 'The work of parents: child care time and costs', unpublished paper.

Doughty, G., Lea, D. and Wedderburn, D. (1978), Addendum in *Lower Incomes*, Report No. 6, Royal Commission on the Distribution of Income and Wealth, Cmnd 7175, London, HMSO.

Doyal, L. and Pennel, I. (1979), *The Political Economy of Health*, London, Pluto Press.

Economist Intelligence Unit (1973), *Care with Dignity: an Analysis of the Costs of Care for the Disabled*, London, National Fund for Research into Crippling Diseases.

Elias, P. (1980a), 'Employment prospects and equal opportunity' in Moss, P. and Fonda, N. (eds), *Work and the Family*, London, Temple Smith.

Elias, P. (1980b), 'The joint distribution of economic activity and earnings of married couples in the UK, 1968 and 1977', paper prepared for the Equal Opportunities Commission, Manchester, EOC.

Equal Opportunities Commission (1980), *The Experience of Caring for Elderly and Handicapped Dependants*, a survey report, Manchester, EOC.

Equal Opportunities Commission (1981), *Behind Closed Doors*, a report on the public response to an advertising campaign about discrimination against married women in certain social security benefits. Manchester, EOC.

Equal Opportunities Commission (1982a), *Caring for the Elderly and Handicapped: Community Care Policies and Women's Lives*, Manchester, EOC.

Equal Opportunities Commission (1982b), *Who Cares for the Carers? Opportunities for those Caring for the Elderly and Handicapped*, Manchester, EOC.

Finch, J. and Groves, D. (1980), 'Community care and the family: a case for equal opportunities?', *Journal of Social Policy*, vol. 9, no. 4, pp. 487–514.

Finch, J. and Groves, D. (1982), 'By women for women: caring for the frail elderly', *Women's Studies International Forum*, vol. 5, no. 5.

Foreman, A. (1977), *Feminity as Alienation*, London, Pluto Press.

Fulbrook, J. (1975), *The Appellant and His Case: the Appellant's View of Supplementary Benefit Appeal Tribunals*, Poverty Research Series 5, London, Child Poverty Action Group.

Garrett, M. (1977), 'Women's work', *Case Con*, issue 25, p. 22.

George, V. and Wilding, P. (1972), *Motherless Families*, London, Routledge & Kegan Paul.

Glendinning, C., *Unshared Care? The Experiences of Parents with a Severely Disabled Child*, London, Routledge & Kegan Paul (forthcoming).

Goldberg, E.M. and Hatch, S. (eds) (1981), *A New Look at the Personal Social Services*, Discussion Paper, no. 4, London, Policy Studies

Institute.

Gough, I. (1979), *The Political Economy of Welfare*, London, Macmillan.

Graham, H. (1982), 'Coping or how mothers are seen and not heard' in Friedman, S. and Sarah, E. (eds), *On the Problem of Men*, London, Women's Press.

Green, S., Creese, X. and Kaufert, J. (1979), 'Social support and government policy on services for the elderly', *Social Policy and Administration*, vol. 13, no. 3, pp. 210-18.

Greenhalgh, C. (1980), 'Participation and hours of work for married women in Great Britain', *Oxford Economic Papers*, vol. 32, no. 2, Clarendon Press, Oxford.

Greenhalgh, C. and Stewart, M. (1981), *Work History Patterns and the Occupational Attainment of Women*, preliminary findings presented to the Manpower Research Group's conference on the National Training Survey, Warwick University.

Hakim, C. (1980), 'New evidence on homeworkers', *Employment Gazette*, vol. 88, no. 10, pp. 1105-110.

Hamill, L. (1978), *Wives as Sole and Joint Breadwinners: Government Economic Service Working Paper, 13*, London, DHSS Economic Adviser's Office.

Harris, A. (1971), *Handicapped and Impaired in Britain*, London, HMSO.

Hartmann, H. (1979), 'The unhappy marriage of Marxism and feminism: towards a more progressive union', *Capital & Class*, no. 8, pp. 1-33.

Hartmann, H. (1981), 'The family as the locus of gender, class and political struggle: the example of housework', *Signs*, vol. 6, no. 3, pp. 366-94.

Horney, K. (1932), 'The dread of women', *International Journal of Psycho-Analysis*, vol. 13, pp. 348-60.

House of Commons (1974), *Social Security Provision for Chronically Sick and Disabled People*, London, House of Commons Paper 276.

Hunt, A. (1968), *A Survey of Women's Employment*, OPCS, London, HMSO.

Hunt, A. (1970), *The Home Help Service in England and Wales*, London, HMSO.

Hunt. A. (1975), *Management Attitudes and Practices towards Women at Work*, London, OPCS.

Hunt, A. (1978), *The Elderly At Home*, OPCS, London, HMSO.

Hurstfield, J. (1978), *The Part-time Trap*, London, Low Pay Unit.

Hyman, M. (1977), *The Extra Costs of Disabled Living*, London, National Fund for Research into Crippling Diseases.

Isaacs, B. (1971), 'Geriatric patients: do their families care?', *British Medical Journal*, 4, pp. 282-86.

Johnson, M.L. (1973), 'Old and young in the family: a negotiated arrangement', paper given at the British Society for Social and Behavioural Gerontology Conference.

Jordan, B. (1976), *Freedom and the Welfare State*, London, Routledge

& Kegan Paul.

Joshi, H. and Owen, S. (1981), *Demographic Predictors of Women's Work Participation in Post War Britain*, London, Centre for Population Studies.

Kamerman, S. B. and Kahn, A. J. (eds) (1978), *Family Policy: Government and Families in Fourteen Countries*, New York, Columbia University Press.

Land, H. (1976), 'Women: supporters or supported?' in Barker, D.L. and Allen, S. (eds), *Sexual Divisions in Society*, London, Tavistock.

Land, H. (1977), 'Social security and the division of unpaid work in the home and paid employment in the labour market' in *Social Security Research*, papers presented at a DHSS seminar on 7–9 April 1976, London, HMSO, pp. 43–61.

Land, H. (1978), 'Who cares for the family?', *Journal of Social Policy*, vol. 7, no. 3, pp. 357–84.

Land, H. (1980), 'The family wage', *Feminist Review*, vol. 6, pp. 55–7.

Land. H. and Parker, R. (1978), 'Implicit and reluctant family policy— United Kingdom', in Kamerman, S.B. and Kahn, A.J. (1978).

Layard, R., Frederking, M. and Zabalza, A. (1980), 'Married women's participation and hours', *Economica*, 47, pp. 427–544.

Layard, R., Piachaud, D. and Stewart, M. (1978), *The Causes of Poverty*, Royal Commission on the Distribution of Income and Wealth, Background Paper No. 5, London, HMSO.

Lee, R.A. (1981), 'The effects of flexi-time on family life—some implications for managers', *Personnel Review*, vol. 10, no. 3, pp. 31–35.

Leete, R. and Anthony, S. (1979), 'Divorce and remarriage: a record linkage study', *Population Trends* 16, London, HMSO.

Leonard Barker, D. and Allen, S. (1976), *Dependence and Exploitation in Work and Marriage*, London, Longman.

Lewenhak, S. (1980), *Women and Work*, London, Fontana.

Liljeström, R. (1978), 'Sweden' in Kamerman, S.B. and Kahn, A.J. (1978).

Lister, R. (1980), 'Taxation, women and the family', in Sandford, C., Pond, C. and Walker, R., *Taxation and Social Policy*, London, Heinemann.

Lister, R. (1981), *Social Priorities in Taxation*, London, Child Poverty Action Group.

Lister, R. and Wilson, L. (1979), *The Unequal Breadwinner*, London, National Council for Civil Liberties.

London Women's Liberation Campaign for Legal and Financial Independence (1978), *The Demand for Independence* (revised edition), London, LWLCLF.

Malos, E. (1980), *The Politics of Housework*, London, Allison & Busby.

Marsden, D. (1969), *Mothers Alone*, Harmondsworth, Penguin Books.

Marsden, D. (1973), *Mothers Alone* (revised edition), Harmondsworth, Penguin Books.

Marsh, A. (1979), *Women and Shiftwork*, London, OPCS.

Martin, J. and Morgan, M. (1975), *Prolonged Sickness and the Return to Work*, OPCS, HMSO, London.

McIntosh, A. (Industrial Facts and Forecasting, Ltd.) (1980), 'Women at work: a survey of employers', *Employment Gazette*, vol. 88, no. 11, pp. 1142-49.

McIntosh, M. (1978), 'The state and the oppression of women', in Kuhn, A. and Wolpe, A.M. (eds), *Feminism and Materialism*, London, Routledge & Kegan Paul.

McIntosh, M. (1979), 'The welfare state and the needs of the dependent family', in Burman, S. (ed.), *Fit Work for Women*, London, Croom Helm.

McIntosh, M. (1981), 'Feminism and social policy', *Critical Social Policy*, vol. 1, no. 1, pp. 32-42.

McNay, R. and Pond, C. (1980), *Low Pay and Family Poverty*, London, Study Commission on the Family.

Mead, M. (1949), *Male & Female*, New York, Morrow.

Ministry of Health (1963), *Health and Welfare: the Development of Community Care*, Cmnd 1973, London, HMSO.

Mitchell, J. and Oakley, A. (eds) (1976), *The Rights and Wrongs of Women*, Harmondsworth, Penguin Books.

Moroney, R.M. (1978), 'The family as a social service', *Child Welfare* 4, pp. 211-20.

Moroney, R.M. (1980), *Families, Social Services and Social Policy*, Washington D.C., US Department of Health and Human Services.

Moss, P. (1980), 'Parents at Work', in Moss, P. and Fonda, N. (eds) (1980).

Moss, P. (1982), 'Community care of young children', in Walker, A. (1982a).

Moss, P. and Fonda, N. (eds) (1980), *Work and the Family*, London, Temple Smith.

Myrdal, A. and Klein, V. (1956), *Women's Two Roles: Home and Work*, London, Routledge & Kegan Paul.

National Council for the Single Woman and Her Dependants (1982), *Newsletter* 106, London, June.

National Insurance Advisory Committee (1980), *Report of the National Insurance Advisory Committee on the question of the extension of title to Invalid Care Allowance to non-relatives*, Cmnd 7905, London, HMSO.

Nelson, L. (1980), 'Household time: a cross-cultural example', in Berk, S.F. (ed.), *Women and Household Labour*, London, Sage.

Nissel, M. and Bonnerjea, L. (1981), *Looking after the handicapped elderly at home: who pays?*, draft mimeo, London, Policy Studies Institute.

Nissel, M. and Bonnerjea, L. (1982), *Family Care of the Handicapped Elderly: Who Pays?*, London, Policy Studies Institute, no. 602.

Oakley, A. (1974), *The Sociology of Housework*, Oxford, Martin Robertson.

Oakley, A. (1980), *Women Confined: Towards a Sociology of Child-birth*, Oxford, Martin Robertson.

Oakley, A. (1981), *Subject Women*, Oxford, Martin Robertson.
Occupational Pensions Board (1981), *Improved Protection for the Occupational Pension Rights and Expectations of Early Leavers*, Cmnd 8271, London, HMSO.
O'Donovan, K. (1979), 'The male appendage—legal definitions of women', in Burman, S. (1979).
Office of Population Censuses and Surveys (1974), *1971 Census, Household Composition*, London, HMSO.
Office of Population Censuses and Surveys (1980a), *Marriage and Divorce Statistics: England and Wales 1978*, Series FM2, no. 5, London, HMSO.
Office of Population Censuses and Surveys (1980b), *OPCS Monitor*, GHS 80/1, Government Statistical Service, London, HMSO.
Office of Population Censuses and Surveys (1981a), *General Household Survey 1979*, London, HMSO.
Office of Population Censuses and Surveys (1981b), *Marriage and Divorce Statistics, England and Wales 1979*, Series FM2, no. 6, London, HMSO.
Oral History (1977), Women's History Issue, vol. 5, no. 2.
Pahl, J. (1980), 'Patterns of money management within marriage', *Journal of Social Policy*, vol. 9, no. 3, pp. 313-35.
Parker, P., Seyd, C., Tennant, R. and Bayley, M. (1981), *Preliminary Findings from Baseline Data*, Neighbourhood Services Project Dinnington, Working Paper.
Parker, R.A. (1980), *The State of Care*: The Richard M. Titmuss Memorial Lecture 1979-80, Joint (J.D.C.) Israel Brookdale Institute of Gerontology and Adult Human Development in Israel.
Parker, R.A. (1981) 'Tending and social policy', in Goldberg, E.M. and Hatch, S. (eds) (1981).
Parker, S. (1980), *Older Workers and Retirement*, OPCS, London, HMSO.
Parsons, T. (1974), 'Age and sex in the social structure', in Coser, R.L. (ed.), *The Family: its Structure and Functions*, London, Macmillan.
Phillips, A. and Taylor, B. (1980), 'Sex and skill: notes towards a feminist economics', *Feminist Review* 6, pp. 79-88.
Pinker, R. (1972), *Social Theory and Social Policy*, London, Heinemann.
Pollert, A. (1981), *Girls, Wives, Factory Lives*, London, Macmillan.
Rich, A. (1980), *On Lies, Secrets and Silence*, London, Virago.
Rimmer, L. (1981), *Families in Focus: Marriage, Divorce and Family Patterns*, London, Study Commission on the Family.
Rimmer, L. and Popay, J. (1982), *Employment Trends and the Family*, London, Study Commission on the Family.
Rose, H. and Rose, S. (1982), 'Moving right out of welfare — and the way back', *Critical Social Policy*, vol. 2, no. 1, pp. 7-18.
Rosenmayer, L. and Kockeis, E. (1963), 'Propositions for a sociological theory of ageing and the family', *International Social Science Journal*, vol. 15, no. 3, pp. 410-26.
Rossiter, C. and Wicks, M. (1982), *Crisis or Challenge? Family Care,*

Elderly People and Social Policy, London, Study Commission on the Family.

Rowbotham, S. (1973) *Hidden from History*, London, Pluto Press.

Rowland, M. (ed.) (1981), *Rights Guide to Non-Means-Tested Social Security Benefits* (fourth edition), London, Child Poverty Action Group.

Royal Commission on the Distribution of Income and Wealth (1979), *Report No. 8, Fifth Report on the Standing Reference*, London, HMSO.

Sainsbury, P. and Grad de Alarcon, J. (1971), 'The psychiatrist and the geriatric patient', *Journal of Geriatric Psychiatry*, vol. 4, no. 1, pp. 23–41.

Sayers, J. (1982), 'Psychoanalysis and personal politics: a reply to Elizabeth Wilson', *Feminist Review* 10, pp. 91–5.

Schaffer, R. (1977), *Mothering*, London, Fontana.

Shanas, E., Townsend, P., Wedderburn, D., Friis, H., Milhoj, P., and Stehoüwer, J. (1968), *Old People in Three Industrial Societies*, London, Routledge & Kegan Paul.

Shimmin, S., McNally, J. and Liff, S. (1981), 'Pressures on women engaged in factory work', *Employment Gazette*, vol. 89, no. 8, pp. 344–49.

Smith, D. (1974), 'Women's perspective as a radical critique of sociology', *Sociological Inquiry*, vol. 44, no. 1, pp. 7–13.

Spring Rice, M. (1981), *Working Class Wives*, London, Virago.

Stacey, M. (1981), 'The division of labour revisited or overcoming the two Adams' in Abrams, P., Deem, R., Finch, J. and Rock, P. (eds), *Practice & Progress: British Sociology 1950–1980*, London, Allen & Unwin.

Stacey, M. and Price, M. (1981), *Women, Power & Politics*, London, Tavistock.

Streather, J. and Weir, S. (1974), *Social Insecurity—Single Mothers on Benefit*, Poverty Pamphlet 16, London, Child Poverty Action Group.

Strong, P.M. (1979), *The Ceremonial Order of the Clinic: Patients, Doctors and Medical Bureaucracies*, London, Routledge & Kegan Paul.

Supplementary Benefits Commission (1980), *Annual Report 1979*, Cmnd 8033, London, HMSO.

Thatcher, M. (1981), Speech to WRVS National Conference 'Facing the New Challenge', Monday 19 January.

Titmuss, R.M. (1963), 'Pensions systems and population change', in Titmuss, R.M., *Essays on the Welfare State* (second edition), London, Allen & Unwin.

Tobin, S.S., and Lieberman, M.A. (1976), *Last Home for the Aged*, London, Jossey-Bass.

Townsend, P. (1962), *The Last Refuge*, London, Routledge & Kegan Paul.

Townsend, P. (1963), *The Family Life of Old People*, Harmondsworth, Penguin Books.

Townsend, P. (1965), 'The effects of family structure on the likelihood of admission to an institution in old age: the application of a general theory', in Shanas, E. and Streib, G., *Social Structure and the Family: Generational Relations*, New Jersey, Prentice-Hall.

Townsend, P. (1981), 'Elderly people with disabilities', in Walker, A. and Townsend, P. (eds), *Disability in Britain*, Oxford, Martin Robertson.

Townsend, P. and Wedderburn, D. (1965), *The Aged in the Welfare State*, London, Bell.

The Treasury (1980), *The Taxation of Husband and Wife* (Cmnd 8093), London, HMSO.

The Treasury (1982), *The Government's Expenditure Plans 1982-83 to 1984-85*, vol. 1 (Cmnd 8494), London, HMSO.

Ungerson, C. (1981), *Women, Work and the 'Caring Capacity of the Community'*, a report of a research review, Social Science Research Council.

Walker, A. (1980), 'The social creation of poverty and dependency in old age', *Journal of Social Policy*, vol. 9, no. 1, pp. 49-75.

Walker, A. (1981a), 'Community care and the elderly in Great Britain: theory and practice', *International Journal of Health Services*, vol. 11, no. 4, pp. 541-57.

Walker, A. (1981b), 'The level and distribution of unemployment', in Bughes, L. and Lister, R. (eds), *Unemployment: Who Pays the Price*, Poverty pamphlet 53, London, Child Poverty Action Group.

Walker, A. (ed.) (1982a), *Community Care: the Family, the State and Social Policy*, Oxford, Martin Robertson/Blackwell.

Walker, A. (1982b), 'Dependency and old age', *Social Policy and Administration*, vol. 16, no. 2, pp. 115-35.

Walker, A. (1982c), 'The meaning of community care', in Walker, A. (1982a).

Webb, A. and Wistow, G. (1982), 'The personal social services' in Walker, A. (ed.), *Public Expenditure and Social Policy*, London, Heinemann.

Wicks. M. (1982), 'Community care and elderly people', in Walker, A. (ed.) (1982a).

Wilkin, D. (1979), *Caring for the Mentally Handicapped Child*, London, Croom Helm.

Williams, I. (1979), *The Care of the Elderly in the Community*, London, Croom Helm.

Woodburn, M. (1973), *The Social Implications of Spina Bifida*, Edinburgh, Scottish Spina Bifida Association, Eastern Branch.

Wright, K.G., Cairns, J.A. and Snell, M.C. (1981), *Costing Care*, Sheffield, University of Sheffield/Community Care.

Wynn, M. (1972), *Family Policy*, Harmondsworth, Penguin Books.

Index